INTERNATIONAL SOCIALISM ★

A quarterly journal of socialist theory

Autumn 1999
Contents

continued overleaf

Autumn 1999
Contents continued

INTERNATIONAL SOCIALISM ★

A quarterly journal of socialist theory

LABOUR LANDSLIDES in Britain, France and Germany have already given way to a profound crisis for the victorious parties. Most dramatically, the Schröder government in Germany has gone from electoral triumph to electoral disaster within a year, losing heartlands in western Germany and being overtaken by the reformed Stalinist PDS in eastern Germany. Alex Callinicos charts the class struggles underpinning these political reverses. These signs of the unpopularity of Blairism internationally can also be read in its country of origin, as the elections to the Scottish Parliament and the Welsh Assembly demonstrated. Michael Lavalette and Gerry Mooney's analysis of the ideology of New Labour shows how deeply anti working class, pro-market sentiment has penetrated the Labour leadership.

KEN COATES has been a longtime labour movement activist, a critic of Blairism and an opponent of the recent Balkan War. In this issue we publish his critique of former peace activists who joined the pro-war lobby. John Baxter welcomes Ken Coates's defence of the anti-war movement, but dissents from the conclusion that the United Nations is a suitably neutral force which can resolve imperial conflicts.

THE MILLENNIUM seems a good moment to examine the event that defines the Christian calendar, the birth of Jesus. John Rose examines the historical evidence for the existence of Jesus in the context of social conflict in the Roman Empire. This theme is continued in Chris Harman's look at the shape of the last century and Mike Gonzalez's review of Tim Clark's book on the dominant art form of the last 100 years, Modernism.

KARL MARX's continuing popularity is confirmed by the widespread acclaim for Francis Wheen's new biography, reviewed here by Peter Morgan. Marshall Berman's *Adventures in Marxism*, reviewed by Anne Alexander, is also a sympathetic study of Marxism. Anna Chen looks at John Newsinger's study of George Orwell, Rob Hoveman reviews Alex Callinicos's new book on social theory, and Chris Harman joins in the debate on art between John Molyneux and Chris Nineham that has appeared in issues 79, 80, 82 and 84 of *International Socialism*.

Issue 85 of INTERNATIONAL SOCIALISM, quarterly journal of the Socialist Workers Party (Britain)

Published December 1999
Copyright © International Socialism
Distribution/subscriptions: International Socialism,
PO Box 82, London E3
American distribution: B de Boer, 113 East Center Street, Nutley,
New Jersey 07110
Subscriptions and back copies: PO Box 16085, Chicago
Illinois 60616
Editorial and production: 020 7538 5821
Sales and subscriptions: 020 7531 9810
American sales: 773 665 7337

ISBN 1 898876 60 6

Printed by BPC Wheatons Ltd, Exeter, England
Typeset by East End Offset, London E3
Cover by Sherborne Design Ltd

For details of back copies see the end pages of this book

Subscription rates for one year (four issues) are:

Britain and overseas (surface):	individual	£14 ($30)
	institutional	£25
Air speeded supplement:	North America	£3
	Europe/South America	£3
	elsewhere	£4

Note to contributors

The deadline for articles intended for issue 87 of
International Socialism is 1 February 2000

All contributions should be double spaced with wide margins.
Please submit two copies. If you write your contribution
using a computer, please also supply a disk, together with
details of the computer and program used.

Reformism and class polarisation in Europe

ALEX CALLINICOS

Europe in the winter of 1999 presents different faces to the world. At the top, the official Europe of national governments and the European Union (EU) is caught up in the usual round of squabbles and scandals—from the Franco-British 'beef war' to the resignation in the face of allegations of corruption of the French finance minister, Dominique Strauss-Kahn— wrapped up in the pompous rhetoric of European construction.

Down below, the picture is very different. Mass discontent with the official Europe of the elites is growing, but it takes contradictory forms. On the one hand, on 16 October, two mass working class demonstrations initiated respectively by the French Communist Party (PCF) and its Italian counterpart, Rifondazione Communista, took place in Paris and Rome. Elsewhere in Europe, the southern Irish boom economy experienced a national nurses' strike, the biggest industrial dispute Ireland has seen since the 1920s. These events reflect the revival of the European workers' movement after the bitter defeats it suffered in the 1980s.

On the other hand, that same month saw two far right ultra-nationalist parties make important breakthroughs in national elections. The Austrian Freedom Party led by Jörg Haider won 22.6 percent of the vote, giving it second place behind the Social Democratic Party. In Switzerland the People's Party also won second place, with 27.2 percent of the vote. Both parties had run vicious racist campaigns against immigrants and asylum seekers. Arguing that these successes reflected a growing nationalist groundswell against economic globalisation and supranational organisations such as the EU and the

United Nations, the US intelligence consultants Stratfor commented that 'Austria and Switzerland seem to us to be an important signal of shifting political forces in the industrial world'.[1]

How do we make sense of this contradictory picture? Which, if any, of the various forces at work in Europe today—official strategies, workers' resistance, far right reaction—represents the dominant trend? How should socialists respond? This article seeks to address these questions, concentrating on France and Germany in particular.

The 1930s in slow motion

A few years ago, at a somewhat earlier stage of this process, Tony Cliff said that observing the 1990s in Europe was like watching a film of the 1930s in slow motion.

We remember the 1930s today chiefly for three events—the onset of the Great Depression in 1929-1931, Hitler's seizure of power in January 1933, and the outbreak of the Second World War at the end of the decade. These events were, of course, closely connected, but they were not bound together by some iron logic that meant the economic slump led inevitably to fascism and imperialist war.

The Wall Street Crash of October 1929 did indeed usher in the most serious crisis in the history of the capitalist system. World gross domestic product fell by 15 percent, while in the two biggest economies, the US and Germany, it dropped by 29.6 percent and 16.9 percent respectively.[2] Economic slump and mass unemployment put enormous pressure on bourgeois political structures that had already been weakened by the First World War and its revolutionary aftermath. The result was a process of social and political polarisation, as vast numbers of both middle and working class people were prepared to consider much more extreme political solutions of both left and right than they would have contemplated previously.

As it happened it was the right, in the shape of the fascists and more traditional authoritarian conservative forces, that emerged victorious from this struggle, as bourgeois democratic regimes toppled like ninepins, particularly in central and eastern Europe.[3] But this was the result of a fiercely fought out and protracted struggle between the forces of right and left on a Europe-wide scale. To take the most important case, the National Socialist seizure of power in 1933 was no preordained event, but the result of a gamble by leading elements in the ruling class that they could use the Nazi mass movement to crush the German working class. As Trotsky pointed out at the time, it could have been defeated had the main workers' organisations—the Social Democratic and Communist parties— been prepared to unite against the fascists.[4]

Even after the terrible defeat suffered by the German labour movement, workers fought back in a series of struggles that could have wrested the initiative from the fascists and the bosses. In February 1934 the attempt of the French right to seize power evoked a united mass response from workers. Out of this came the impetus for the election of a Popular Front government in May 1936 that was swiftly followed the following month by a great wave of mass strikes and factory occupations. That same summer Spanish workers met General Franco's attempt to overthrow the Popular Front government that had been elected there with revolutionary risings.

What prevented these great workers' movements from shifting the balance of forces sharply to the left was the politics of the Popular Front, preached in particular by the Communist parties, which demanded that the class struggle be restrained for fear of scaring off the 'progressive', 'democratic' wing of the bourgeoisie. So the gains made by the June 1936 occupations were soon thrown away, while the Spanish Revolution was crushed, allowing Franco and his fascist allies to rule Spain for a generation. In June 1940, after the Nazi conquest of France, the same parliament that had been elected with a Popular Front majority voted full powers to Marshal Pétain's Vichy collaborationist regime.

To say that Europe in the 1990s resembles the 1930s in slow motion is not to say that history is repeating itself: most obviously, the economic stagnation that continental Europe has suffered over the past decade is much less severe than the Great Depression. Nor is it to predict the same outcome to the present crisis. Rather, as I put it in 1994:

> *The same ingredients are present today* [as were operative in the 1930s]—*deep seated economic crisis which puts increasing pressure on the social structures which built up during the boom, crisis also of the political system, class polarisation involving both the growth of the fascist right and greater working class militancy. The pace of development of the crisis along these different dimensions, however, is—as yet—slower than it was in the 1930s.*[5]

Germany and the onset of the crisis

When this analysis was first formulated in the early 1990s, the most important developments supporting it were in Germany and Italy. Reunification in 1990 proved paradoxically to be both the moment when Germany re-emerged as a world power and the beginning of the most serious economic crisis the country has experienced since the 1930s. The roots of this crisis lay much deeper than reunification. Germany and the other major European economies have been suffering a deep seated crisis of profitability and competitiveness, reflected throughout the 1980s in slow growth and high unemployment. Reunification briefly masked these underlying problems as massive state spending aimed at incorporating East Germany into the Federal Republic stimulated a short lived boom. But in late 1991 the Bundesbank, worried about the huge surge in government borrowing required to finance the higher spending, sharply raised interest rates, killing off the boom.[6]

Given the central economic position German capitalism has occupied in Western Europe since the late 1940s, the result was to transform Germany from a pillar of stability into a disruptive factor within the EU. The destabilising effects were felt first through the currency gyrations of 1992-1993 within the European Exchange Rate Mechanism (ERM), and then in the harsh monetarist convergence criteria won by the Bundesbank in exchange for replacing the Deutschmark with the euro. Throughout the 1990s Germany, and with it the rest of continental Europe, have experienced slow growth, if not outright recession. This contributed to a widespread sense of malaise, of 'Eurosclerosis', reflecting what many commentators and business leaders felt was the failure of the EU to maintain its competitive position compared to a restructured and apparently reinvigorated US capitalism.

The effect of this continent-wide economic crisis was domestic class polarisation. Articulating the fears of a business class that felt under increasing pressure from its rivals in North America and East Asia, Chancellor Helmut Kohl told the German Bundestag in April 1993, 'With ever shorter working hours, rising wage costs, and ever longer holidays, our competitiveness is in danger. The simple fact is that a successful industrial nation cannot allow itself to be organised like a collective leisure park'.[7] In other words, the gains German workers had won during the 'long boom' of the 1950s and 1960s were to be sacrificed in order to restore the competitiveness of German capitalism.

This offensive seriously undermined the institutionalised structures of social bargaining between the state, capital and labour that had been a distinctive feature of 'Rhineland capitalism' since the Second World War. Kohl's drive to make workers pay the huge costs of reunification by holding down wages provoked a national public sector workers' strike in April-May 1992 and a rash of smaller scale disputes in the key metal industry in 1992-1994.[8] This process of class polarisation involved, however, more than rising working class militancy. Encouraged by a racist climate stirred up by the ruling coalition against asylum seekers, various fascist organisations sought to exploit mass unemployment in both western and eastern Germany. The result was a series of Nazi outrages against foreigners in Rostock, Mölln and Solingen in 1992-1993.

It wasn't simply Germany that was stalked by the spectre of fascism in the early 1990s. The final days of the corrupt and discredited Mitterrand regime in France facilitated the further growth of Jean-Marie Le Pen's National Front. Worse still, the collapse of the post-war Italian parliamentary regime in the *Tangentopoli* scandal swept to office in May 1994 a coalition headed by the right wing media tycoon Silvio Berlusconi, and including five ministers from the National Alliance, as the fascist MSI had renamed itself. Economic and political crisis was polarising politics to the right as well as the left.

France 1995: the turning point

Developments over the past five years have confirmed this analysis. Indeed, the second half of the 1990s has seen the process of class polarisation develop and deepen in two crucial respects. First, workers have won a number of significant victories. Secondly, and partly as a result, politics in Europe has shifted to the left, bringing social democratic parties to office throughout the EU.

The decisive event in this process is undoubtedly the public sector strikes in France of November-December 1995. The attempt of the new right wing regime of President Jacques Chirac and his prime minister, Alain Juppé, to force through a package of neo-liberal 'reforms' designed to prepare France for the euro provoked the biggest upsurge of the French working class since May 1968. As Jim Wolfreys showed in his excellent article in the last issue of this journal, the strikes and the defeat of the 'Juppé Plan' pushed French society significantly to the left.[9]

The following comments by three left wing sociologists highlight how the 1995 strikes allowed working class people to recover confidence in their ability to take collective action after the atomisation and despair of the Mitterrand years:

> *The first achievement of the struggle wasn't the preservation of gains but the defatalisation of the policies pursued for two decades, the conviction that one could fight them successfully. In other words, the first conquest of the strike movement is the strike itself... In the course of its development the mobilised actors experienced their own strength, they realised that it is possible to do 'something else', they discussed problems such as social protection that are supposed to be 'complicated', reserved normally only for specialists. This was a labour of massive and frontal contestation of the unstated defining assumptions of neo-liberalism which overwhelmed everyone taken individually but which enriched itself within the collectivity as it deliberated. In the strikers' general assemblies, speech circulated freely, or better, liberated itself: 'The strike is like champagne; it removes inhibitions'.*[10]

A wave of strikes and other social struggles—for example, by the *sans-papiers* (immigrants denied official documents)—followed in the wake of autumn 1995. By April 1997 the Parisian daily *Libération* could declare that 'strikes...are blossoming like mushrooms in the thunderstorm of the crisis'.[11] That same month, in yet another desperate gamble, Chirac dissolved the National Assembly. The ploy badly backfired: the 'plural left' coalition of the Socialist, Communist, and Green parties won the legislative elections. This was an astonishing reversal given that only four years earlier the right wing parties had won a landslide victory thanks to popular revulsion against the Socialist Party under Mitterrand. After that earlier defeat the Socialist former prime minister Pierre Beregevoy had shot himself in despair. Now Lionel Jospin rode the wave unleashed by the 1995 strikes back to office.

Faced with this shift to the left, the National Front was thrown into crisis and suffered a damaging split. Meanwhile, at the intellectual and cultural level, the reactionary climate which had set in during the late 1970s with the emergence of the anti-Marxist *nouveaux philosophes* began to disintegrate. In particular, the renowned sociologist Pierre Bourdieu stepped forward to attack neo-liberalism and to champion the 'social movements' of 1995 and after. Coming after two decades in which leading intellectual figures such as Foucault and Baudrillard had broken with the left and pored scorn on collective action, this was an important shift. As the Trotskyist philosopher Daniel Bensaïd wrote of Bourdieu, in 'turning his symbolic and cultural capital against the dominant discourse of expertise and competence...he re-legitimises a speech of resistance'.[12] Bourdieu's interventions contributed to a broader critique of globalisation which, while expressed largely in left reformist terms, represented a sharp break with '*la pensée unique*'—the neo-liberal consensus of the 1980s and early 1990s.

The French strikes of November-December 1995 marked a turning point at a European level as well. In their way, they were as significant as the defeat of the British miners' strike of 1984-1985. If the Great Miners' Strike symbolised the ability of ascendant neo-liberalism in the shape of its most aggressive and self confident representative, Margaret Thatcher, to crush even the best organised and most militant workers, the French strikes suggested that a new page was being turned in the history of the Western labour movement. The neo-liberal offensive was provoking a popular reaction capable of unleashing massive social struggles out of which working class militants could begin to rebuild organisationally and politically from the defeats of the 1980s.

Europe swings left

If France was the high point, there were other important struggles elsewhere. The Berlusconi coalition, for example, evoked a huge response from the Italian working class. In December 1994 a general strike shut the country down, and an enormous trade union demonstration swept over Rome. Faced with this resistance, the government rapidly disintegrated.

In Germany the Kohl government's offensive ran into the ground. In September 1996 the ruling conservative-liberal coalition forced a package of cuts through the Bundestag, including a cut in sick pay to 80 percent. This was a gauntlet thrown at the organised working class. West German workers had won the right to 90 percent, later 100 percent, sick pay as a result of a 114 day strike by steel workers in 1956-1957. The government's initiative gave the green light to an aggressive group of employers led by Jürgen Schrempp, boss of Daimler-Benz. Schrempp had been pushing for a style of management much more like the Anglo-American model of deregulated free market capitalism. His strategy for Daimler involved the globalisation of investments (reflected in the company's subsequent merger with Chrysler) and maximising 'shareholder value'—stock marketese for short term profits. He rammed through the cut in sick pay straight away (Kohl had promised the change would apply only to new contracts). But Schrempp had miscalculated. The fury of rank and file workers forced a fierce reaction from IG Metall, the metal trade union. Faced with a wave of strikes centred on Daimler's Bremen works, the bosses had to back down.

This defeat was simply the most decisive episode in a much broader wave of resistance to the Kohl government. For example, in June 1996 the DGB (the German TUC) organised an enormous demonstration against Kohl's cuts in the federal capital, Bonn. Attempts to move nuclear materials provoked massive confrontations between riot police and thousands of protesters. At the end of 1997 students mounted a nationwide wave of occupations and demonstrations. A piece published in *Wirtschaftswoche*, the German equivalent of *The Economist*, vividly evokes the atmosphere in the last days of the Kohl government:

> *Eggs crack on pavements, and fireworks explode. Thousands of miners besiege the government quarter in Bonn in defence of state subsidies for their industry... Strange scenes take place in the besieged headquarters of the FDP* [the liberal junior partner in the Kohl government]. *One liberal politician turns up at a window, holds up his champagne glass and sticks two fingers up at the miners. Germany 1997, a new whiff of class struggle...*
>
> *This sleepy republic has never been so lively. Not a day goes by without someone somewhere taking to the streets for or against something! First there were the anti-nuclear demonstrations, then the miners, and then the building*

workers. This week it's the steel workers' turn... There is no doubt that things
are beginning to move in this country. The rising voices of protest demonstrate
this clearly. Fasten your seat belts, dear readers, it's going to get extremely
turbulent!...

No political commentator in recent years has got it as wrong as Francis
Fukuyama, who, after the collapse of really existing socialism in Eastern
Europe, declared the 'End of History', claiming that capitalism had finally and
decisively beaten all 'competing ideologies'. Socialism might have failed eco-
nomically, but as a political ideal it is turning out to be extremely hard to kill.[13]

This process of class polarisation was not confined to Western Europe.
Canada, with its strong trade unions and relatively developed welfare
state, is in many respects closer in social structure to Western Europe than
to the US. In 1994 a right wing Tory administration headed by Mike
Harris won office in Ontario and mounted a determined assault on the
welfare state. This provoked a series of one day city-wide general strikes
throughout the province, the most industrialised part of the country. At its
high point in October 1996, 1 million workers went on strike in Toronto,
with 300,000 marching through one of North America's leading cities.

In the end this campaign was shut down by the leaders of the Ontario
Confederation of Labour, allowing Harris to win re-election in 1999. The
Canadian strikes, like the major European struggles, have been bureaucratic mass strikes, called and controlled by trade union leaders, though in
some cases (notably the French strikes) there was a considerable degree
of rank and file initiative involved as well. This did not alter the significance of what was happening: workers were beginning to recover their
confidence, even if they usually were still reluctant to act independently
of the trade union bureaucracy.

The main exception to this pattern was, of course, Britain. The defeats
suffered by British workers during the 1980s had been much more severe
than in any other major European country. However bitter they might
have felt, rank and file workers lacked the confidence to act independently, while a deeply demoralised trade union leadership did everything
it could to prevent strike action taking place in the desperate hope that the
election of a Labour government would allow it to win the concessions
for which it was unwilling to fight. The huge wave of anger that swept the
country in the autumn of 1992, after Tory economic policy collapsed with
the pound's expulsion from the ERM and the government announced the
closure of most remaining pits, could have led to a revival in workers'
struggles. This possibility vanished as the miners' leader Arthur Scargill
lined up with the TUC General Council to block any attempt to mount
direct action. Nevertheless, 1992 did mark a turning point.
Disillusionment with the failure of Thatcherite 'popular capitalism' drove
millions of working class people into the reformist camp. It was this,

rather than Tony Blair's personal magnetism or New Labour's policies, that laid the basis for the Labour Party's huge election victory on 1 May 1997.[14]

Labour's triumph was simply the most dramatic instance of the political reversal that took place in the second half of the 1990s. The mass rejection of neo-liberalism found political expression in a wave of electoral victories for social democratic parties. Greece led the way, reflecting the intensity of social conflict in that country since the mid-1980s. After fierce class battles under the right wing Mitsotakis government in the early 1990s, Andreas Papandreou's PASOK was returned to office in 1993. The disintegration of the Berlusconi coalition paved the way for the victory of the Olive Tree coalition, dominated by the PDS (the Party of the Democratic Left, formerly the Communist Party), in the Italian general elections of April 1996.

In 1997-1998 the pace speeded up. First came the election of the first Labour government Britain had seen in 18 years. Then came the unexpected triumph of the 'plural left' in the French legislative elections of May-June 1997. Finally, the German federal elections at the end of September 1998 brought the Social Democratic Party (SPD) back to office for the first time in 17 years. The defeat of Helmut Kohl, the longest serving German chancellor since Bismarck, allowed Gerhard Schröder to form a 'Red-Green' coalition. In the aftermath, the *Financial Times* found itself ruefully weighing the consequences of what it called 'Europe's Red October', now that 'the centre-left is back in power in 13 of the EU's 15 states'.[15]

The French and German electoral victories took place in a significantly different context from that in Britain. Blair's path to office was smoothed by the memory of shattering defeats suffered by the British working class in the 1980s. Demoralised activists were willing, more or less reluctantly, to accept New Labour policies as the price of victory. But in Germany, as we have seen, the working class remains strong and undefeated. Kohl's failure to deliver the neo-liberal 'reforms' demanded by big business meant that in the run-up to elections the German establishment put their hope in a tied result. This would then permit the formation of a 'Grand Coalition' of the SPD and the CDU (Christian Democratic Union, the main conservative party) to force through these 'reforms'.

In the event, the swing to the left was far too pronounced for this. In Schröder the SPD chose a chancellor candidate very much in the Blairite mould. He underlined his pro-business credentials, having, as state premier of Lower Saxony, served on Volkswagen's supervisory board, and had himself photographed ostentatiously smoking a cigar to recall images of Ludwig Erhard, the CDU architect of the 'economic miracle' of the 1950s. Schröder's spin doctors coined the slogan of *Die neue*

Mitte—the new centre—to indicate his break with traditional social democratic politics.

But the atmosphere in German society forced to the SPD in the course of the campaign to place its main emphasis on what amounted to an 'Old Labour' programme of social reform. This reflected the character of the SPD itself as a traditional social democratic party with deep roots in a strong organised working class based in one of the biggest and most successful industrial economies in the world. Perry Anderson noted:

> The SPD is not in thrall to its chancellor. It is a very different party from New Labour. Twice the size, with 700,000 individual members, its culture remains noticeably working class. The atmosphere of an SPD rally in any big industrial town is closer to Labour meetings of the 1960s or 1970s than to anything in Britain today.[16]

This was reflected in the fact that the SPD chairman was *not* Schröder, but Oskar Lafontaine, left reformist state premier of the Saarland, a powerful orator trusted by the party rank and file. Having won the party leadership after the SPD's last defeat in 1994, Lafontaine conceded to the media friendly Schröder the chancellor candidacy in order to ensure electoral victory in 1998. But he continued to express his vocal opposition to free market economics, writing a book with his wife called *Don't Be Afraid of Globalisation*. Anderson predicted optimistically soon after the Red-Green coalition was formed, 'As minister of finance, and chairman of the SPD, his position in the new regime is unusually strong. Lafontaine is the first Western politician of aggressively Keynesian outlook in 25 years'.[17]

Lafontaine's apparently powerful position in the new government was indicated by the decision of Schröder's nominee for economics minister, the successful computer entrepreneur Jost Stollman, to bow out during the preliminary coalition negotiations, complaining that the government was going to be more left wing than he had expected. Moreover, the participation of the Greens brought into the foreign ministry Joschka Fischer, a veteran of the Frankfurt far left in the 1960s and early 1970s. The media declared that the generation of the 1960s had taken office.

The new government was thus a coalition in more than one sense, since it involved not merely the Reds and the Greens, but, within the SPD itself, the dual leadership of Schröder and Lafontaine. The left wing character of the government was underpinned by an apparently significant electoral shift. In the 1994 federal elections Kohl had been saved by the support for the CDU in the 'new *Länder*' in eastern Germany. By 1998, however, the experience of economic collapse had turned the east against Kohl. This benefited not merely the SPD, but also the Party of

Democratic Socialism (PDS)—the old Stalinist ruling party in East Germany, which had successfully converted itself into a left reformist organisation that took over 20 percent of the vote in the east in 1998. The combined share of the vote of the SPD, Greens and the PDS was 60.3 percent in the east, compared to 50.6 percent in the west. Anderson observed, 'What we are looking at, then, is the potential emergence of a long run sociological majority for the left in Germany'.[18]

Similarly in France, Jospin had to respond to a political climate reflecting considerably more working class militancy than Blair had to deal with. He was therefore careful to differentiate himself from the Blairite 'Third Way'. Jospin declared himself in favour of 'a market economy' but not 'a market society'. Soon after taking office he said, 'If market forces are allowed to let rip, it will spell the end of civilisation in Western Europe'.[19] Jospin's 'plural left' coalition government included not merely the Greens but the PCF, which is, rhetorically at least, much further left, for example opposing the euro. The centre of gravity of the new governments in France and Germany was thus well to the left of New Labour.

Lafontaine's fall, Schröder's crisis

Yet the past year has exposed the fundamental contradiction in the revival of European social democracy: brought to office by mass rejection of neo-liberal policies, the reformist governments have nonetheless continued with these policies. This contradiction is most flagrant in Britain where, within days of taking office, Blair and his Chancellor of the Exchequer, Gordon Brown, conceded a fundamental monetarist demand by giving the Bank of England control over interest rates.

The phenomenon is, however, much more general. The commitment of social democracy to administering the existing system was clearly demonstrated during the Balkan War, when the German and French governments proved themselves to be as determined supporters of NATO's bombing campaign as Tony Blair or Bill Clinton. Blair was able to boast that this was a war waged by 'a new generation of leaders in the United States and in Europe...who hail from the progressive side of politics'.[20] Indeed, despite Blair's posturing, French aircraft were more heavily involved in the bombing than the Royal Air Force. Joschka Fischer even proclaimed the war an anti-fascist struggle like the Spanish Civil War.

Moreover, on 11 March 1999, shortly before the outbreak of the Balkan War, Lafontaine suddenly resigned as finance minister and SPD chairman. His departure opened the door for the Red-Green government to shift towards a New Labour agenda. Symbolically enough, Schröder was on the way to a press conference to launch the German edition of

Anthony Giddens's Blairite tract *The Third Way* when he learned of Lafontaine's resignation. No sooner was the war over than Blair and Schröder launched a policy document entitled *The Third Way/Die neue Mitte*. Drafted by Peter Mandelson and his German counterpart Bodo Hombach, it called for a neo-liberal package of welfare 'reforms', 'flexible' labour markets and the like.

Schröder followed this up with an effort to show big business that he would cut the massive almost DM1,500 billion government debt he had inherited from Kohl. In June 1999 Lafontaine's successor as finance minister, Hans Eichel, unveiled a package of DM30 billion (£10 billion) of impeccably Thatcherite spending cuts. Pensions would rise in line with the rate of inflation, and not, as previously, the increase in earnings. Civil service pay would be similarly capped, while corporation tax would be cut from 35 to 25 percent.

This reversal reflected determined pressure from the ruling class. From the start, the bosses and the right wing parties mounted concerted opposition to key reforms. The first such case was provided by the new government's effort to reform a racist citizenship law inherited from the Wilhelmine era that ties nationality to German descent. The government's proposal to extend citizenship to those of foreign descent by allowing for dual nationality was challenged in particular by Edmund Stoiber, state premier of Bavaria and leader of the CDU's ultra-conservative Bavarian partner, the Christian Social Union (CSU). Bucking the national trend, the CSU won an absolute majority in the 1998 Bavarian state elections using the slogan, 'Germany is not a country for immigrants.' Stoiber mounted a vicious campaign against the dual nationality bill. He threatened a 'march on Berlin' and cleverly appealed to mass discontent over economic issues such as employment. Thus Stoiber attacked what he called the 'caviar faction', who supported the new law while ignoring ordinary people and their problems.

In February 1999, marking the beginning of a disastrous cycle of reverses at the polls, the Red-Green governing coalition lost the state elections in Hessen (which includes the key financial centre of Frankfurt). This was rapidly followed by a government retreat over dual nationality, led by Lafontaine. Schröder declared that the government must avoid 'minority subjects'. Soon afterwards a promise to phase out nuclear power stations was abandoned, with Schröder publicly overruling the Green environment minister, Jürgen Trittin.

But much more spectacular, and apparently decisive, was the fall of Lafontaine. The *Financial Times* greeted his appointment as finance minister with apprehension as marking 'the return of neo-Keynesian economics'.[21] As soon as he took office Lafontaine launched a public campaign to persuade the Bundesbank and the European Central Bank to cut European interest rates. The Red-Green coalition took office at a crucial conjuncture—the financial panic of autumn 1998 and the launch of the euro in January 1999. The tight money policies pursued by the Bundesbank since 1991 and generalised throughout Europe by the convergence conditions for the euro kept Germany, and therefore continental Europe, in recession for much of the 1990s. The president of the European Central Bank, Wim Duisenburg, promised a continuation of these policies. His reaction to the autumn 1998 panic was to deny that there was a crisis: 'We will see about a crisis if that event arrives'.[22]

In line with his Keynesian outlook, Lafontaine pushed hard for interest rate cuts to revive the European economy. He also argued that target zones linking the major currencies—the dollar, the yen, and the euro—would secure greater global financial stability. Despite the fact that elsewhere central banks were following the lead of the US Federal Reserve Board and cutting interest rates, Duisenberg and the Bundesbank fiercely resisted Lafontaine's demands. The supposedly 'neutral' and 'independent' ECB made its political point by waiting till April 1999, *after* Lafontaine's resignation, before cutting interest rates by half a percentage point.

Lafontaine also infuriated British Tory Eurosceptics by calling for EU tax harmonisation, provoking the famous front page in *The Sun*, 'Is This The Most Dangerous Man In Europe?' German bosses would have undoubtedly replied, 'Yes.' Their ire was provoked by Lafontaine's plans to lighten the tax burden on the mass of wage earners, and thereby to promote higher consumer spending that would help revive the economy. As part of this package he proposed scrapping corporation tax reliefs. This proposal absolutely enraged German big business. Leading companies threatened to move their operations abroad. A remarkable article by the veteran *Financial Times* journalist John Plender in early March 1999 was headlined 'Bosses To The Barricades'. Plender quoted a study by the Institute for Fiscal Studies which showed that the tax burden on German big business was relatively light: 'In mid-decade, Germany had the lowest level of corporate income tax revenues as a percentage of gross domestic product in the group of seven leading industrial countries.' The furious reaction reflected a broader feeling by Germany's bosses that they were under pressure—thus many had been angered by the relatively generous 3.6 percent pay increase won by metal workers in February. Plender explained:

The revolt is, in reality, as much about clipping Mr Lafontaine's wings as tax. Business and the stock market are concerned that he is enfeebling corporate Germany and damaging the credibility of the European Central Bank with his ineffectual economic policies and crude lobbying for lower interest rates. A letter leaked this week revealed that a group of 22 bosses has been trying to persuade Gerhard Schröder...to rein in the maverick and unreconstructed minister.[23]

Within a week of that article appearing Lafontaine was out of office. His resignation was so abrupt that it invited speculation that either personal or political blackmail had been involved. But whatever the precise mechanics of Lafontaine's downfall, as the *Financial Times* rightly put it, 'The leaders of German industry have claimed their scalp.' The paper compared the affair with Mitterrand's U-turn in the early 1980s, when, under pressure from the financial markets, he abandoned the left-Keynesian platform on which he had been elected and replaced it with neo-liberal policies: 'Mr Mitterrand's government had two years in power before executing its *volte face*. Mr Lafontaine concertina'd that process into little more than four months before his politics met the combined resistance of the European Central Bank and German businesses threatening to switch to locations elsewhere'.[24]

After Lafontaine's fall the Red-Green coalition seemed set firmly on a Blairite course. Schröder's two key initiatives in June 1999, in the immediate aftermath of the Balkan War—the joint policy document he signed with Blair and the spending cuts package—reflected his confidence in his ability to pursue the politics of *die neue Mitte*. He took over the party chairmanship and imposed his own candidate as SPD general secretary. Within the government Schröder's hand was strengthened by the evolution of the Greens under Fischer's leadership towards the espousal of aggressively neo-liberal policies.

This proved, however, to be a false dawn for the German version of the Third Way. Ironically for a chancellor selected for his vote winning qualities, Schröder suffered a series of devastating electoral defeats after Lafontaine's resignation. First came the European parliamentary elections in June 1999, where the SPD's vote fell to 30.7 percent, 1.5 percentage points lower than its performance in the previous elections in 1994 and over 10 points lower than its share of the votes in the federal elections nine months before. The CDU/CSU's share soared to 48.7 percent of the poll. Then, in the early autumn of 1999, the SPD lost no less than five successive state elections. Four of these polls took place in eastern states where voters had swung massively to the SPD in 1998. Anderson's 'long run sociological majority for the left' seemed to be withering on the vine. But the disaster wasn't confined to the east. Lafontaine's old stronghold of the Saarland, on the French border, also fell to the right wing tide. And in municipal elections in the largest state, North Rhine Westphalia, the CDU became the leading party in such traditional SPD strongholds in the industrial Ruhr as Dortmund, Düsseldorf and Cologne. Schröder's personal popularity plummeted till he was trailing behind his conservative rival in the opinion polls. He faces the real possibility of losing the next federal elections in 2002. In the short term the electoral defeats mean the government has lost control of the upper chamber of the German parliament, the Bundesrat, which is composed of state representatives. The CDU now has a veto over many government policies.

It would, however, be too simple to see the Red-Green coalition's electoral collapse as reflecting a swing to the right in German society. True, in the arena of national bourgeois politics the CDU has been the main beneficiary. Nazi parties have also made some important gains. Thus the fascist Deutsche Volksunion won 5.3 percent of the vote in Brandenburg. But the polarisation has been to the left of the SPD as well. The PDS won 23.3 percent of the vote in Brandenburg, up five points on the previous election. It forced the SPD into third place in Thuringia and increased its vote in Berlin to 17.8 percent. The PDS is a complicated formation. It retains the loyalty of a section of the east German middle class, based mainly in the public sector, who feel their situation has deteriorated since reunification. Unlike the SPD, it lacks any organic links with the trade unions. But this has given the PDS leadership the freedom to present itself as significantly to the left of the SPD (though when in state coalition governments with the SPD it pursues essentially the same policies as the social democrats). Nevertheless, the left wing positions the PDS takes (for example, it was the only parliamentary party that opposed the Balkan War) have allowed it to pick up the votes not merely of disgruntled working class people, but of radical youngsters in the west.

The successes achieved by the PDS indicate that the main driving force in the SPD's electoral collapse has been the bitterness and disillusionment caused by Schröder's failure to break with Kohl's policies. In August 1999, 4.1 million people were unemployed, 10.5 percent of the workforce—a higher figure than when the Red-Green coalition took office. Many working class voters have reacted to the absence of real change by staying at home or voting for the PDS.

The same impatience has been reflected within the SPD as well. The Blair-Schröder document and the cuts package provoked widespread anger among party and trade union activists. Forty left wing SPD deputies issued a statement denouncing Schröder's 'reforms', and demanding a restoration of the link between pensions and earnings and the reintroduction of the wealth tax that Kohl had scrapped in 1997. The government was forced onto the defensive. 'We have spent the whole summer talking about the injustices of the savings package,' finance minister Eichel ruefully admitted.[25]

Schröder's situation was exacerbated when Lafontaine emerged from his self imposed silence to denounce the government's new course. In an interview in late September 1999 in the *Welt Am Sonntag* newspaper he blamed the election defeats on the SPD's failure to continue with his economic policies. Lafontaine followed this up with a book, *The Heart Beats on the Left*, in which he gave an insider's view of the first few months of the Red-Green government and denounced Schröder's politics and leadership style. This assault provided a focus within the workers' movement for left wing opposition to New Labour style policies. Meanwhile, the sharp shift to the right by the Green leadership was provoking bitter opposition from party activists.

By October, a somewhat punch drunk Schröder seemed to be wondering publicly whether he had been right to hitch up to the Blairite bandwagon. On a television talk show he conceded that it had been a mistake to rush out his joint policy document with Blair without any internal party discussion. SPD general secretary designate Franz Münterfering played down the document's significance, saying that it had no 'direct concrete consequences' for government policy.[26] Behind the difficulties confronting the Red-Green coalition lies the fundamental fact that it had to deal with a relatively strong and undefeated workers' movement. The highly intelligent neo-liberal commentator Martin Wolf summed up the problem when he reviewed the prospects for the government after Lafontaine's resignation. Criticising Schröder for abandoning many of Kohl's free market 'reforms', Wolf nevertheless discounted the possibility of his successfully pursuing Blairite policies: 'Under the liberalising alternative a left of centre German government would introduce even more radical reforms than those it has already reversed. This will not happen. It is all very well for Tony Blair to suggest it should. But even his government is merely the beneficiary of its predecessor's efforts'.[27]

In other words, to borrow another formulation of Tony Cliff's, Schröder has to be both the German Thatcher *and* the German Blair. Blair has been able to build on the Tories' successes in weakening the organised working class. Schröder, by contrast, confronts a working class with no such recent memory of bitter defeat—indeed, a class whose militancy has been growing in recent years. This puts important limits on his freedom of action. Hence even the joint document with Blair stresses the importance of 'partnership' between workers and bosses in the shape of Schröder's Alliance for Jobs with the trade unions (formulations to which Mandelson strongly objected). Despite the ties of loyalty binding German workers to the SPD and therefore to the government, Schröder will encounter massive resistance if he seeks seriously to dismantle the welfare state. He faces a task of Herculean proportions.

Polarisation within the reformist camp

These developments in Germany are one instance of a more general phenomenon in Western Europe—*polarisation within the reformist camp*. The new social democratic governments have generally failed to break with the neo-liberal policies of their right wing predecessors. Nevertheless, because these governments were brought to office by a shift to the left in society at large, usually reflecting a revival in workers' struggles, the disillusionment produced by their policies has not caused a simple swing of the pendulum back to the right, or even to the far right. There have been some gains for fascist or semi-fascist parties—most notably in the Austrian and Swiss elections. These represent, however, more a warning for the future than an immediate threat.

The dominant feature of the present situation is rather a process of division that is taking place among the supporters of the reformist government, in which a section of the working class begins to look further to the left. This can be seen even in Britain. Though the Tories won the Euro elections, they did so not because of a revival of their popularity (on the contrary, under William Hague's leadership they moved fast towards becoming a loony right ultra-Thatcherite nationalist party), but because of massive abstentions by traditional Labour voters. In the Scottish and Welsh elections in May 1999 New Labour came under severe pressure from nationalist parties presenting themselves as more left wing than the government: heartland Labour seats in the mining valleys of the Rhondda fell to Plaid Cymru, while the Scottish Socialist Party won a seat in the new parliament in Edinburgh.

The same process is much more developed on the continent. As we have seen, in Germany disillusionment with Schröder has taken the form of both polarisation within the SPD itself and a swing by voters to the PDS. But it is in France, where the mass radicalisation has been greatest, that social and political tensions have become most pronounced. Despite his more radical rhetoric, Jospin's policies have often not been that different in practice from those of Schröder or Blair. A mildly Keynesian economic policy has allowed public spending to rise to boost domestic demand and counteract the effects of the Asian and Russian crises. But in June 1999 the *Financial Times* could comment, 'The Jospin government has been able to privatise more in two years than any of its predecessors, even selling off flagship state entities such as Air France and France Telecom'.[28]

As for the government's key reform, the introduction of a 35 hour week, the journalist Robert Graham commented on the revised bill unveiled that same summer by the social affairs minister, Martine Aubry, 'The new law incorporates major concessions to business.' For example, within an overall annual ceiling of 1,600 working hours per employee, 'Companies can negotiate with unions over how these hours are to be spread over the year. Already this is becoming a lever to introduce changes in work patterns.' Thus Carrefour, the biggest supermarket chain, has used the law to introduce such 'Anglo-Saxon' productivity raising practices as teamworking:

'The company chooses not to emphasise the word, but the 35 hour week has enabled it to introduce flexibility in all but name'.[29]

Jospin—a much cleverer politician than either Blair or Schröder—has nevertheless been much more careful to use traditional social democratic language to keep his supporters happy. Thus he ostentatiously refused to endorse the Blair-Schröder document. His caution reflects the climate of social conflict that reigns in France today. The struggles unleashed by 1995 have not ceased under Jospin. Thus barely had he been elected than he had to confront a highly embarrassing wave of occupations mounted by unemployed activists and their supporters.[30] Different struggles and movements have proliferated. Twice in the past six months, for example, high school students have taken to the streets in their hundreds of thousands.

This social ferment has produced a revitalised and diverse left. One political scientist distinguished no less than four lefts around the government. The first, 'social-liberal', grouping, represented by the right wing of the Socialist Party, accepts the neo-liberal *pensée unique*: it is the closest thing in France to the Blairite Third Way. But this tendency is much weaker and more isolated than its British or even its German counterparts. The second, 'neo-Keynesian', grouping supports Jospin's own position, summed up by the ambiguous slogan, 'Yes to the market economy, no to the market society.' Thirdly, there are 'national republicans' like interior minister Jean-Pierre Chévènement, leader of the Mouvement des Citoyens, and the philosopher Régis Debray, who champion French national sovereignty against the US, the EU and multinationals (both opposed the Balkan War, though Chévènement did not resign from the government). Finally, there is the 'radical' left—the Communist Party, Bourdieu, the main far left organisations Lutte Ouvrière and the Ligue Communiste Révolutionnaire, the militant SUD (Solidaires, Unitaires, Démocratiques) unions, and various activist coalitions supporting the *sans-papiers*, the unemployed, and so on.[31]

As this description shows, the revived left involves more than formal political groupings and organisations. A plethora of different single issue campaigns have grown up in the past few years. There are also various journals, notably the monthly *Le Monde diplomatique*, and intellectual groupings—for example, Raisons d'agir, founded by Bourdieu in December 1995—which help to sustain a critique of neo-liberal 'globalisation'. This is a climate where opposition to what is seen as the US-dominated World Trade Organisation (WTO) and support for measures to regulate global financial markets—for example, the so called Tobin Tax on speculative transactions—is growing. Groupings such as the Association pour la taxation des transactions financières et l'aide aux citoyens (Attac), supported by both left reformists and the far left, and some trade union leaders, are campaigning against any extension of the

World Trade Organisation's powers.

At the same time, French capitalists are increasingly asserting themselves. Even if the big firms can use the Aubry law introducing the 35 hour week to their advantage, small and medium employers lack the same room for manoeuvre. And the climate described above creates pressure for reforms that represent unwelcome restrictions on all French bosses' freedom of action. Ignoring the parliamentary conservative parties, still in profound disarray after successive electoral routs, the French employers have been taking direct action: a claimed 25,000 bosses marched through Paris on 4 October to protest against the 35 hour bill.

Caught between pressure from an increasingly angry and militant bourgeoisie, and the various left wing currents and workers' organisations, Jospin has been forced to tack and turn. At the beginning of September, Michelin caused a furore by announcing 7,500 redundancies. On 13 September, Jospin told a television interviewer that his government could do nothing about large scale job cuts announced by Michelin: 'You can't expect everything from the state,' he said.[32] Within barely a fortnight, the angry reaction within the workers' movement had forced Jospin to withdraw this confession of impotence. Unveiling a new government programme, he declared: 'Globalisation doesn't make states impotent. Economic policies can have a major impact on economic developments... *The state must arm itself with new instruments of regulation, adapted to the realities of capitalism today'.*[33]

Later that autumn, the growing social and political tensions over the Aubry law spilled over onto the streets, first with the bosses' demonstration on 4 October. The left's riposte came on 16 October, as 60,000 responded to the Communist Party's call to demonstrate against unemployment. This call represented a gamble on the part of the PCF leader Robert Hue. The *Financial Times* might praise him as 'a model of compromise', but the PCF still had to maintain control of its working class base.[34] In the Euro elections the PCF share of the vote fell to just under 7 percent, while the Greens took 10 percent, and the joint list of Lutte Ouvrière and the Ligue Communiste Révolutionnaire won 5 percent.

Faced with this challenge from the left the PCF had to demonstrate its strength—particularly since the CGT, the trade union federation long associated with the party, refused to back the 16 October march. In the event the gamble paid off, as PCF supporters dominated a large and confident working class demonstration that also included sizeable contingents from the far left. But—reflecting the other face of Hue's strategy—the day before the demonstration PCF deputies in the National Assembly voted for a revised version of the Aubry law that embodied only minor concessions to the left. Aubry's spin doctor claimed, 'The amendments are not the fruit of haggling since the equilibrium of the text has been perfectly preserved'.[35]

The polarisation over the Aubry law suggests that there will be more social confrontations. Having taken to the streets once, the bosses may seek to move onto a wider offensive. They may, however, find themselves blocked by the response from the organised working class. Fuelled by higher public spending, the French economy is projected to grow by 2.8 percent next year. According to the *Financial Times*, this 'should be higher than Germany and Italy, the other two big eurozone economies, which have been harder hit by the Russian and Asian crises and have been slower to recover'.[36] Relatively high growth is likely to boost the confidence of a workers' movement that has enjoyed significant victories in the past few years. The French bourgeoisie will not find it easy to regain the initiative.

Left reformist challenges to the main social democratic parties have also emerged elsewhere in Europe. In Italy Rifondazione Communista, whose core support comes from former Communist Party activists who opposed its transformation into the PDS, won 8.6 percent of the vote in the 1996 parliamentary elections.[37] In Greece, where since becoming prime minister in 1995 Costas Simitis has pursued New Labour style policies, the 1999 European elections saw voters react strongly. PASOK's share of the vote fell to 32.9 percent of the vote, behind the conservative New Democracy's 36.3 percent. Three left reformist parties, however, saw their votes rise. The Communist Party won 8.5 percent of the vote, DIKKI, a left wing breakaway from PASOK 6.9 percent, and the ex-Communist Left Coalition 5 percent. Between them the three parties now have seven MEPs compared to PASOK's nine.[38]

Conclusion

The growth of left reformism is no reason for complacency. Whether within established social democratic parties or organisationally separate from them, it represents a revival of the politics of traditional reformism—of what Blair likes to denounce as 'Old Labour'. This is a politics that failed when to put the test during the earlier stages of the present period of crises in the 1970s and 1980s, whether under Harold Wilson and James Callaghan in Britain, Willy Brandt and Helmut Schmidt in West Germany, or François Mitterrand in France. Lafontaine's abrupt resignation after a few months of media attacks was hardly heroic when one considers the intense vilification that Tony Benn suffered for ten years, let alone the fate of Salvador Allende, who died fighting in his presidential palace. Indeed, the affair highlighted the fundamental weakness of reformist politics—namely its reliance on a state apparatus that capital can bend to its will. Therefore the calls put forward by Jospin and Lafontaine for the 'regulation' of capitalism hardly amount to a serious challenge to an economic system whose inner logic drives it towards exploitation and crisis.

This does not alter the significance of the process of polarisation described above. The experience of neo-liberal policies has pushed the working class throughout Europe back towards social democracy. The failure of the resulting governments to abandon their predecessors' policies has produced a further reaction, in which a section of workers want to go further. This has breathed new life into left reformism. Even though the solutions it offers are quite inadequate, the resulting debates are of immense importance. There is a sense in which the Blairites, by going on the ideological offensive and seeking to force the pace of 'modernisation' on a European scale, have helped to feed the reaction to the left. Key New Labour texts such as Giddens's *The Third Way* and the Blair-Schröder document have become a focus of debate right across Europe. Moreover, social radicalisation has stimulated the emergence of more militant left reformist currents—most notably that associated with Bourdieu in France. The result is the emergence of analyses and arguments that in certain respects—in particular the critique they involve of deregulated liberal capitalism—converge with those of the classical Marxist tradition. This represents an important opportunity for revolutionary socialists to break out of the intellectual isolation in which they have been confined for the past two decades, provided that they engage with these currents in a way that is both sympathetic and, where necessary, critical.[39]

It is therefore crucial that revolutionary socialists intervene in these debates. This requires more than producing theoretical critiques of the Third Way, though these are important. More concrete initiatives are also required, depending on the strength and circumstances of the organisation concerned. For example, the sister organisation of the SWP in Germany, Linksruck, has intervened strongly in support of Lafontaine's challenge to Schröder around the slogan 'Oskar is right'. The Socialist Workers Party in Britain is campaigning in support of Ken Livingstone's bid to become Labour candidate for mayor of London: the Labour Party leadership's attempts to block him have made him a focus for discontent with New Labour.

The starting point for such initiatives has to be unity against the bosses and against right wing social democracy. This does not mean, however, that support for left reformist challengers such as Lafontaine and Livingstone can be uncritical (particularly in the light of the latter's support for the Balkan War). On the contrary, within the framework of unity against Blair, Schröder and their ilk, friendly arguments should be raised about the limits of left reformism: thus Linksruck criticises Lafontaine for advocating the regulation of capitalism rather than its replacement by a socialist planned economy based on workers' control. Where this fits the situation of the organisation concerned, revolutionary socialists should be willing to take their challenge to both right and left social democracy into the electoral arena. Thus the Greek Socialist Workers Party (SEK) ran a slate in the Euro elections of June 1999, while the British SWP stood candidates in the Scottish and Welsh elections: both these initiatives enjoyed modest successes that justified the experiment (the Irish SWP has also made some successful electoral initiatives in recent years).

Whatever form it takes, it is essential that revolutionary socialists move to take advantage of the opportunities offered by the polarisation within the reformist camp. The metaphor of 'the 1930s in slow motion' implies that the pace of the crisis is slower today than it was during the Great Depression. In my original analysis, I stressed the reasons for this difference—most notably that the economic crisis today is still far less severe than it was in the 1930s, bourgeois democracy has much stronger social roots in continental Europe than existed in the inter-war era, and the fascist parties have so far been more successful at winning votes than building mass paramilitary movements.[40]

But the film of the 1930s is running, albeit more slowly. The cumulative effect of long term economic stagnation and mass unemployment—the jobless rate in Germany and France seems stuck at between 10 and 12 percent, condemning millions to poverty and despair—is putting enormous pressure on existing social and political structures. If a credible left wing alternative does not emerge, then disillusionment with social democracy's capitulation to the market, particularly if it coincides with the next world recession, will strengthen the far right. The National Front in France, for example, is weakened, but far from finished. The Austrian and Swiss elections are thus a timely warning. Revolutionaries can and must make a decisive difference to whether such a real socialist alternative does develop.

Notes

1   www.stratfor.com, 'Austria, Switzerland and the Politics of Nationalism', *Global Intelligence Update: Weekly Analysis*, 1 November 1999, p5.

2   A Maddison, *Dynamic Forces in Capitalist Development* (Oxford, 1991), Table 4.1, p87.

3   The fragility of liberal democracy after 1918 is well evoked by Mark Mazower in his otherwise disappointing history of the 20th century Europe, *Dark Continent* (London, 1998).

4   L D Trotsky, *The Struggle Against Fascism in Europe* (New York, 1971).

5   A Callinicos, 'Crisis and Class Struggle in Europe Today', *International Socialism* 63 (Summer 1994), p39.

6   See C Harman, 'Where is Capitalism Going?', part 1, *International Socialism* 58 (Spring 1993), pp30-33; and A Callinicos, op cit, pp14-21.

7   *Financial Times*, Survey on Germany, 25 October 1993.

8   See A Callinicos, op cit, pp24-29.

9   J Wolfreys, 'Class Struggles in France', *International Socialism* 84 (Autumn 1999); see also C Harman, 'France's Hot December', *International Socialism* 70 (Spring 1996); and S Beroud et al, *Le Mouvement social en France* (Paris, 1998).
10 S Beroud et al, op cit, pp119-120.
11 *Libération,* 4 April 1997.
12 D Bensaïd, 'Desacraliser Bourdieu', *Le Magazine littéraire*, October 1998, p69. See, more generally, A Callinicos, 'Social Theory Put to the Test of Politics: Pierre Bourdieu and Anthony Giddens', *New Left Review* 236 (July-August 1999).
13 *Wirtschaftswoche*, 30 March 1997.
14 See L German, 'Before the Flood?', *International Socialism* 61 (Winter 1993).
15 *Financial Times*, 24 October 1998.
16 P Anderson, 'The German Question', *London Review of Books*, 7 January 1999.
17 Ibid.
18 Ibid.
19 *Financial Times*, 7 June 1997.
20 T Blair, 'We are Fighting for a New Internationalism', *Newsweek*, 19 April 1999.
21 W Munchau, 'Return To Keynes', *Financial Times*, 26 October 1998.
22 *The Guardian*, 14 October 1998.
23 J Plender, 'Bosses To The Barricades', *Financial Times*, 6 March 1999.
24 *Financial Times,* 13 March 1999.
25 R Atkins, 'Lonely In The Middle', *Financial Times*, 14 September 1999.
26 *Financial Times*, 5 October 1999.
27 M Wolf, 'The German Disease', *Financial Times*, 17 March 1999.
28 *Financial Times*, 9 June 1999.
29 R Graham, 'Turning Back The Clock', *Financial Times*, 29 July 1999.
30 See Beroud et al, op cit, pp174-184.
31 L Bouvet, 'Quartre, elles sont quartre', *Le Monde*, 10 October 1999.
32 *Libération,* 28 September 1999.
33 www.premier-ministre.gouv.fr, 'Intervention du Premier ministre aux Journées parlemenaires du Groupe socialiste', 27 September 1999, p8.
34 *Financial Times*, 9 June 1999.
35 *Le Monde*, 17 October 1999. See also a similar assessment in D Mezzi, 'Construire un nouvel elan de mobilisation', *Rouge*, 21 October 1999.
36 *Financial Times*, Survey on World Economy and Finance, 24 September 1999.
37 See T Behan, 'The Return of Italian Communism?', *International Socialism* 84 (Autumn 1999).
38 *Financial Times*, 15 June 1999.
39 See my discussion of Bourdieu in A Callinicos, 'Social Theory Put to the Test of Politics', op cit, pp85-102.
40 A Callinicos, 'Crisis and Class Struggle in Europe Today', op cit, pp37-43.

New Labour, new moralism: the welfare politics and ideology of New Labour under Blair

MICHAEL LAVALETTE AND GERRY MOONEY

Introduction

The landslide victory for the Labour Party at the May 1997 general election represented a dramatic rebuff of 18 years of Tory policies. From 1979, when Thatcher was first elected, there was a gradual erosion of the welfare state, with council house sell offs and the introduction of the market into the health service and education system. Revulsion against the visible decline of the welfare state was part of the reason why millions voted Labour in May 1997. Yet after two years of New Labour in government there is increasing dissatisfaction with its welfare programme which has continued many of the Tories' themes. Benefit cuts have been implemented or threatened against lone parents, those on disability allowances and the elderly. Money that has gone into schools and hospitals has been inadequate to meet the needs of these services and has been tied to the implementation of what Blair has termed 'best business practices'. The problem of underfunding in education is to be 'solved' by appointing roving 'super-teachers' who will drop into schools and instruct teachers and pupils in 'appropriate' teaching methods and discipline codes. While in the NHS new hospitals being built are to be funded out of the Private Finance Initiative—ensuring that private companies will be guaranteed 'profits from illness'. Although the national minimum wage was implemented in April 1999 the rate really was minimal—leaving many workers working for poverty pay. The sense of crisis within the welfare system remains significant as more users witness declining services in the face of the privatisation onslaught.

Against this background New Labour has used social welfare policy to assert a new moral agenda. Towards the end of 1999 this increasingly focused on the problem of teenage pregnancy. As *The Guardian*'s leader noted on 6 September:

> *Blair has put 'moral' on the masthead* [of government policy]. *And for all his fine talk of modernising Britain it is clear his understanding of that loaded word is saloon-bar suburban: it means sex...*[but his]*...'moral' does not...cover sex at large... Moral mean* [sic] *to him what it did to Octavia Hill in the 1880s: the evils of poor people fornicating.*[1]

In practice this is little different from Major's 'back to basics' or the policy prescriptions of some of the most right wing Tories during the Thatcher years.

The consequence is an increasingly vicious attack on poor working class communities. Working class kids on desolate housing estates have been criminalised and are subject to night time curfews, or threatened with jail for a range of 'anti-social misdemeanours', such as the two 17 year olds in Liverpool who face a possible five year sentence if they are caught spitting in public, among other things.[2] Working class families have been informed that they will be held responsible for any crimes or misdemeanours their children may undertake. Those on a range of benefits have been told that work is their 'salvation', even if it means working for benefits, and that unemployment is not an option.

Wrapped up in the rhetoric of New Labour is a claim that all these welfare developments are both positive and new, the 'Third Way', based on a communitarian ethic of guaranteed citizens' rights obtained in return for responsibilities to the nation, an attempt to modernise Britain, its institutions and attitudes, to become a dynamic enterprise-based economy for the 21st century. But lurking within New Labour's policies is a vicious ideology which both demonises and victimises some of the very poorest sections of the working class, that blames the poor and their 'individual inadequacies' for their situation rather than the structural constraints of more than 20 years of mass unemployment and welfare cuts. In this article we focus on the welfare policies and ideology of New Labour and its consequences for Britain's poor.

The New Labour project

In the period following the 1997 general election considerable attention has been devoted to examining and dissecting the Blair project. The emphasis which New Labour places on style and presentation, together with Blair's pragmatism and eye for the populist selling point, often obscures the thrust of Labour policies. With New Labour there appears to be a complex mixture of disparate and often contradictory statements, viewpoints and policy announcements. In the field of social and welfare policy this has been evident with, on the one hand, attacks on single parents, the disabled and welfare dependency, and on the other, the introduction of more progressive income tax family credits, the introduction of a national minimum wage, albeit at a very low level, and, after widespread protests against the Labour government's early announcements about benefit cuts, the decision in the 1998 budget to maintain universal child benefit. Despite this, the ideological and political thrust of New Labour is clear.

During its time in opposition Labour politicians were often very vocal in their attacks on the Tory record on poverty and inequality. While some of the party's leading figures, such as Frank Field—once described by right wing Tory MP and shadow welfare spokesman David Willets as the Tories' 'favourite Labour politician'—could be relied upon to embrace some aspects of Conservative thinking on poverty, many Labour MPs claimed that tackling poverty was the most important objective of a Labour government. Even Tony Blair admitted in 1996, 'I believe in greater equality. If the next Labour government has not raised the living standards of the poorest by the end of its time in office it will have failed'.[3]

Before we consider these claims in more detail let us first of all examine the New Labour project, in which social and welfare policies play a pivotal role.

The first point to make is that while Blair and his colleagues have made great play of Labour's policies as ones which will effectively modernise and renew Britain, the ideas upon which they are based are hardly new. Since becoming Labour leader in July 1994, Blair has consistently emphasised his Christian beliefs and values and how these influence his policies. His Christianity also underscores his understanding of socialism and his rejection of Marxism as a rigid, deterministic perspective:

The problem with Marxist ideology was that, in the end, it suppressed the individual by starting with society. But it is from a sense of individual duty that we connect the greater good and the interests of the community—a principle the church celebrates in the sacrament of communion.[4]

The socialism of Marx, of centralised state control of industry and production, is dead. It misunderstood the nature and development of a modern market economy: it failed to recognise that the state and public sector can become a vested interest capable of oppression as much as the vested interests of wealth and capital; and it was based on a false view of class that became too rigid to explain or illuminate the nature of class division today.[5]

Blair's caricature of Marxism owes more to 1980s and 1990s sociology textbooks than it does to an informed grasp of Marxist ideas. This account of Marxism, however, serves its purpose in the development of Blair's alternative, which he terms 'ethical socialism'. This approach does not seek to suppress the individual to the power of the state, as Blair depicts Marxism doing, but sees the individual as paramount. While there are direct lines connecting this view with classical liberal social and political thought, Blair differs from liberalism in his claim that individuals are 'socially interdependent' beings and thus individual self interest 'is inextricably linked to the interests of society'.

This perspective, which Blair calls 'social-ism', is one which he sees as pivotal in the New Labour project and informs many of the policies which Labour has enacted. The principles of ethical socialism, he argues, will support the key tasks of the Labour government, 'intervening to equip and advance the individual's ability to prosper within this new economy'.[6] Thus Blair's ethical socialism embraces neo-classical supply-side economics which emphasise self investment in 'human capital' as cornerstones in the fight against unemployment. Alongside this stress on the 'socially interdependent' individual is an emphasis on two notions which have long been central to conservative thought, 'community' and 'family':

History will call it the Decent Society, a new social order for the Age of Achievement for Britain. We will respect family life, develop it in any way we can, because strong families are the foundations of strong communities.[7]

One influence on Blair is the Scottish religious philosopher John Macmurray. Writing in the early part of the 20th century, Macmurray argued that individual fulfilment could only be found in communities of intense personal relationships where people were bound together by mutual obligations. It was the individual's (Christian) duty to meet those obligations placed on them, primarily through helping others. For Blair, 'the search is on to reinvent community for a modern age, true to core values of fairness, co-operation and responsibility'.[8]

Another source of New Labour thinking on community has been the moral communitarians in the United States. 'Communitarianism' has become a popular and influential way of describing political and ideological appeals to community and community values on both sides of the Atlantic. For proponents of communitarian ideas, these appeals rest on a rejection both of the market-led ideology of the new right and of paternalistic and centralised state approaches to welfare of the 'old left'. Thus communitarianism is viewed by its advocates as steering a path between unfettered markets and an overarching state. The most populist moral communitarian commentator of the 1990s was the American sociologist Amitai Etzioni. For Etzioni, societies like the US and Britain are faced with problems of 'demoralisation'—a decline in morality and the absence of a commitment to fulfilling obligations: 'Communitarians call to restore civic virtues, for people to live up to their responsibilities and not merely to focus on their entitlements, and to shore up the moral foundations of society'.[9]

For Etzioni, the key to the remoralisation of society is based upon the strengthening of morality in and through civil institutions such as the family, education system and voluntary associations; the assertion of public/community interest over special interests; and the reversal of the problem of 'too many rights, too few obligations'. Or, as Blair put it in an interview in the ever virtuous *Sun* in early 1998, Britons need to 'stop wringing their hands and start taking more responsibility for their own lives'.

New Labour's stress on moral communities is all too evident in its approach to crime. Here is Tony Blair in the aftermath of the murder of Liverpool toddler James Bulger:

> *I have no doubt that the breakdown of law and order is intimately linked to the break up of a strong sense of community. And the break up of community in turn is, to a crucial degree, consequent on the breakdown in family life. If we want anything more than a superficial discussion on crime and its causes, we cannot ignore the importance of the family.*[10]

The notion of a breakdown in law and order, however, is difficult to sustain. Recent analysis of crime statistics suggests there was a decrease in recorded crime in England and Wales in the late 1980s and early 1990s.[11] This has produced a subtle shift in terminology. Increasingly talk is of 'anti-social behaviour', which means acts which break the law but do not necessarily lead to the culprits getting caught or prosecuted.[12] In the hands of New Labour supporters and ministers the term 'anti-social behaviour' can be applied to a range of activities from infringement of legal codes to 'morally unacceptable behaviour'. It panders to some of the most reactionary ideas in society about poor working class communities as a pool of lawlessness and moral depravity. For David Blunkett it means that 'those committed to a 21st century welfare state have to cease paternalistic and well meaning indulgence of thuggery, noise, nuisance and anti-social behaviour'.[13]

In an increasing number of Labour councils across Britain where

Blairites are influential, a stronger line is being taken against 'anti-social activities', with tenants having to sign new contracts with authorities committing them to a variety of activities, from keeping gardens 'neat and tidy' to looking after children 'properly'. Where tenants are deemed to be failing in their duties and obligations, the threat of eviction hangs over them. If this fails there is always the sanction of more direct policing via curfews. On one working class estate in Hamilton (just outside Glasgow), Strathclyde police have maintained a dusk to dawn curfew for under 16s for over a year, a policy which a number of Labour's leaders argue should be repeated elsewhere.[14] Indeed, in August and September 1999 Blair argued that local authorities and police forces were not using their powers against 'anti-social elements' with anything like the vigour they should. As he put it, 'Twelve year old children should not be on the street at night'.[15] Of course, Blair does not mean all children: it is poor children in inner city areas or desolate council estates who instil fear and loathing, and the focus on these 'problem children' is part of the wider attack on the 'moral malaise' of this section of the 'community'.

For New Labour, 'community' is closely intertwined with a second notion, 'family'. Despite Labour's much acclaimed recognition of difference and diversity in social and family life, the implicit conservatism of its social policy project is again very evident. As Jack Straw stated in 1996:

> the absence of prejudice should not mean the absence of rules, or order, or stability... Let our social morality be based on reason—not bigotry. But let us not delude ourselves that we can build a society fit for our children to grow up in without making a moral judgement about the nature of that society... Any decent society is founded on duty [and] responsibility. A philosophy of enlightened self interest in which opportunity is extended...[leads to] greater security, safer streets, motivated young people.[16]

In Labour's green paper on welfare reform (1998) Frank Field, another of New Labour's committed Christians, shows less acceptance of family diversity:

> The family is the bedrock of a decent, civilised and stable society. But it is under enormous strain. Divorce and separation have increased, lone parenthood has risen and child poverty has worsened. The reasons for this may be varied, but the impact is clear: more instability, more crime, greater pressure on housing and social benefits.
>
> **A fundamental principle of the welfare state should be to support families and**

children. But the way of doing that today must change. The shape of the family has changed significantly in recent decades. But families remain the building block of society.

Changes in society mean that parental separation is becoming less exceptional. By providing parents, children and families with great support, our policies may help to stem the tide of family breakdowns.[17]

Interestingly, recent opinion polls suggest most people reject these values. *The Observer* of 25 October 1998 found that only 8 percent of people thought ministers could be trusted to talk sense on family matters (with agony aunts and Catholic priests scoring better!); two thirds of respondents thought single parents could bring up children as well as couples; and only 15 percent thought government policy and benefits should favour married couples over lone parents.

Nevertheless, 'family values' have filtered into a range of welfare pronouncements. We have already noted New Labour's insistence that anti-social behaviour is a consequence of bad families. For David Blunkett, Secretary of State for Education and Employment, it is also the cause of educational failure:

Where there is a problem, it is all too often because parents claim not to have the time, because they have disengaged from their children's education or because, quite simply, they lack even the basics of parenting skills... With such a lack of expectation [reinforcing] generations of disadvantage...it is the poverty of expectation and dedication which is the deciding factor [in educational failure].[18]

Jack Straw wants parenting classes to be accepted in the same way as ante-natal classes, though such classes will also involve compulsory counselling and guidance classes for parents ordered by courts to receive help dealing with their 'delinquent' children.[19]

New Labour, then, has not been short on appeals to return to 'family values', particularly when the issues of crime, parenting and education have been the topic of discussion. The consequence is that a range of religious, communitarian and more conservative themes are brought together in a highly moralistic stew of censure, condemnation and punishment. But the diverse influences on New Labour do not end here. We have already noted the way in which the Labour government has become closely identified with public relations, presentation and style. The media have frequently focused on the role of 'spin doctors'. These spin doctors are, however, also involved with networks of intellectuals and policy makers, who strive to provide New Labour with some intellectual basis and who are closely involved with the Labour leadership in developing the New Labour project.

New Labour and the search for a Third Way

Much has been made in the press of the 'special relationship' which
Tony Blair shares with President Clinton in the US. The reasons for this
are not difficult to detect and are largely a product of Blair's approval of
the policies pursued by the Clinton government in the 1990s. Much of
the media attention has been on Labour's adoption of the image making
and marketing strategies of the Democratic Party in the US. Notable here
is New Labour's desire to distance itself from 'Old Labour' and the traditional institutions of the Labour Party, particularly the trade unions. In
place of trade union and labour movement officials and activists, New
Labour has increasingly relied upon the services of 'non-partisan' political advisers and public relations experts, freelancers who move around
political parties as the political climate ebbs and flows. The new breed of
spin doctors are in control of 'information management', ensuring that
policy announcements are in tune with the findings of numerous focus
groups and telephone canvassing. Again, as with the Democrats, Labour
has increasingly sought to canvass and embrace the views of sections of
finance and big business, employing leading business people on consul-
tancies and as directors of a variety of projects such as Welfare to Work
and the Low Pay Commission. While trade union leaders were given
what union leader Ken Jackson termed a 'bollocking' by Blair at a
meeting in Downing Street in September 1998, the New Labour door has
always been open to business representatives.

Blair is further supported by 'policy entrepreneurs' organised in a
variety of left of centre think tanks, such as the Institute for Public Policy
Research (IPPR), Demos and Nexus. It is through the work of these
organisations, and academics such as sociologist Anthony Giddens and
Geoff Mulgan, Demos director and former stalwart of *Marxism Today*,
that we can trace some of the sources of other US influences in ways
which are less to do with style and more to do with ideological drive.

This drive is reflected in Blair's commitment to basing New Labour
on the politics of the Third Way. The Third Way has been the focus of
considerable academic and political discussion in Britain since Blair's
policy discussions with Bill Clinton in February 1998 seemed to initiate
a new Atlanticist economic and social policy. On his return from the US
he spoke of the need to create a new politics which was distinct from
both the Old Left and new right. In doing so Blair and New Labour
embraced a perspective which was heavily influenced by Clinton and a
range of Democratic policy advisers. This is a view which takes globalisation as given and argues there is little that individual economies can do

except run with the flow of the world economy, pursuing those policies which would give a competitive edge such as greater labour market flexibility and tight controls on public expenditure, particularly on 'wasteful' welfare payments.[20] Thus the state can no longer be expected to redistribute income and wealth nor to modify the worst excesses of the market.

The Third Way is, however, an extremely slippery notion and there is little agreement even amongst Blair's supporters as to what it consists of. Giddens argues that the Third Way represents a renewed social democracy for the new world of globalisation and rampant individualism. It relies upon a commitment to a new mixed economy where markets are *regulated*, not controlled, by the state and where rights are matched by responsibilities for both business and the individual.

The overall aim of Third Way politics should be to help citizens plot their way through the major revolutions of our time: globalisation, transformations in personal life and our relationship to nature. Third Way politics should preserve a core concern with social justice, while accepting that the range of questions which escape the left/right divide is greater than before. Freedom to social democrats should mean autonomy of action, which in turn demands the involvement of the wider social community. Having abandoned collectivism, Third Way politics looks for a new relationship between the individual and community, a redefinition of rights and obligations.[21]

The Third Way, whatever it actually means, represents the clearest sign of New Labour's abandonment of class as a meaningful notion for understanding how society works. While Blair and other leading Labour politicians claim that Britain is a classless society, the notion of class they employ is largely a psychological one, similar to that embraced by Thatcher. While she maintained that class would disappear if people stopped talking about it, Blair argues that 'class distinctions are unhelpful and divisive' and that 'class-bound' politics belong to the world of 'Old Labour'.[22] It is left to Blairite supporters such as Giddens to provide some intellectual justification for such a view: 'With the rapid shrinking of the working class and the disappearance of the bipolar world, the salience of class politics, as well as the traditional divisions of left and right, has diminished'.[23]

For New Labour, British society has changed qualitatively from the days when the old welfare state was at its highpoint. New Labour frequently invokes the radically changing world to provide a basis not only for its attack on the two failed pasts of the state and the market,[24] but to add legitimacy to its arguments and policies today. Speaking in the journal of the Labour Co-ordinating Committee, Robin Cook claims:

Tony Blair has made an invaluable contribution to the Labour Party in transforming it into the party of change rather than the party that is opposed to change. An integral part of the crisis for the left during the Thatcher years was that we were transformed into the political force that defended the postwar settlement. As a result, we became trapped into a political culture that was defensive—even, ironically, conservative. By contrast, Thatcherism in part succeeded in capturing support because it conveyed an image of thrusting radical change.[25]

What are these changes? In addition to the emphasis on globalisation and the inability of states to moderate its effects, Labour's leaders now claim there have been a number of irreversible socio-economic developments in the world over the last 20 years. They suggest that the labour market is dominated by flexibility, information processing, new working patterns, and a greater reliance on knowledge and education, with the consequence that there are no longer jobs for life. Thus the neo-liberal labour market agenda, the drive for greater flexibility, is one which has to be supported if the British economy is to compete effectively.[26]

The main consequence of this, according to Blair, is that ideologies based upon a 'particular economic prescription' or on a 'time-limited view of class', Blairspeak for Marxism, have become 'historically redundant'. But it means also that institutions and systems developed for the 'old world' are now in need of reform, and none more so than the welfare state:

Reform is a vital part of rediscovering a true national purpose, part of a bigger picture in which our country is a model of a 21st century developed nation: with sound, stable economic management; dynamism and enterprise in business; the best educated and creative nation in the world; and a welfare state that promotes our aims and achievements.

But we should not forget why reform is right, and why, whatever the concerns over individual benefits, most people know it is right. Above all, the system must change because the world has changed beyond the recognition of Beveridge's generation...We need a system designed not for yesterday, but for today.[27]

Thus for Blair, New Labour is above all a 'modernising project' underpinned by a pragmatism which transcends the 'old' ideological battles. Central to this project is the reformation of the whole welfare state.

New Labour's welfare programme

Labour's desire to reform the welfare state was much in evidence before

Tony Blair became Labour leader. In 1992, then leader John Smith set up the Commission on Social Justice in an effort to reformulate Labour's welfare policies. The main report of the commission—*Strategies for National Renewal*—involved an effective retreat from some of the central aspects of the post-1945 welfare state, particularly in relation to collectivism and the pursuit of equality, which it now called social justice. The report acknowledged that there was a growing social polarisation between rich and poor in Britain, but at the same time suggested that greater inequality was inevitable while simultaneously embracing the Tory view that welfare spending was a drain on resources.

Thus, in anticipation of Blair's soundbite machine, the commission's reports have all the key catchphrases of welfare reformers, such as, 'The welfare state must offer a hand-up rather than a handout,' and that it should be transformed 'from a safety net in times of trouble to a springboard for economic opportunity'.[28] The report is also strong on the need to attack what the Tories consider to be the primary problem with welfare, 'dependency'. Again, in anticipation of some of the Labour government's subsequent statements, the commission called for intelligent regulation and fair flexibility in the labour market, attempting to marry greater levels of productivity with improved working conditions. Importantly the commission drew a distinction between three types of policy approaches: 'deregulators' who advocate the free market, 'levellers' who call for the redistribution of income, and 'investors' who call for redistribution of opportunity as well as income. In identifying with the latter approach, the Commission on Social Justice set the scene for much of Blair's welfare reforms, albeit without the commitment to redistribution of income.

Looking back to the Commission on Social Justice after the first two years of the Labour government it is clear how far New Labour has travelled under Blair. Like the Tories before it, Labour has argued the need to reform the welfare system, emphasised the costs of welfare, and has accepted the notion that the old social security programme was doing little to tackle the causes of poverty. What is the evidence for the increased costs of welfare? If we consider welfare spending as a share of total national income, there is remarkable stability in the share going to welfare. In 1995-1996 welfare spending amounted to 26 percent of GDP, the same as it was 20 years before. On social security spending there *has* been an increase, from 8.2 percent of GDP in 1973-1974 to 11.4 percent in 1995-1996—more than double in real terms, but this is a direct result of increases in levels of poverty and unemployment as well as longer term demographic factors.[29] The government's own Social Trends report in 1998 shows that spending per head on welfare benefits is very low, with Britain ninth out of 11 in the European table of spending on social benefits. The report also shows that 90 percent of the population now think that more money should be spent on welfare benefits and public spending. However, Labour, like the Tories, blames the victims of poverty by claiming they are 'welfare dependent'. The attack on welfare dependency has been a key part of the new right assault on state provision over the last decade. Together with that other catch-all term, the underclass, welfare dependency sits alongside fraudulent claimants, scroungers and welfare junkies as the pivotal reasons why Labour sees the welfare system as in need of reform.

How have such ideas been imported into New Labour's agenda? One of the most obvious sources here is Frank Field. Giving Field the key post of minister for welfare reform in his first government says much about Blair's own perspectives on welfare, and while Field has resigned from this position his thinking remains influential in New Labour circles, notably through his successor, Alistair Darling. While starting as one of the founding members of the Low Pay Unit and director of the Child Poverty Action Group in the early 1970s, Field is now associated with some of the most right wing thinking on welfare in Britain. He is a regular contributor to reports by the right wing policy grouping the Institute of Economic Affairs (IEA).[30] This may seem a long way to shift politically, but even in the 1970s Field's right wing views were evident in his calls for the sale of council housing, and, since the early 1990s, he has been a strong advocate of private pension provision. But one of his key concerns is his desire to regulate and police the benefits system much more forcefully and to increase checks on those suspected of not looking hard enough for work, or working and signing on.

In his book *Making Welfare Work* (1995) and in his various publications for the IEA,[31] Field embraces many of the views of the right wing US social scientist Charles Murray.[32] For Murray, welfare spending has led to the growth of a welfare dependent underclass who live on the margins of society. Chief among the behaviours of the so called underclass which Murray (and Field) deplore and condemn most forcefully are: illegitimacy, family breakdown, criminal behaviour, and the lack of a work ethic. In the past Field's own perspective on the underclass stressed the role of structural factors such as rising unemployment and demographic and household changes in creating exclusion,[33] but his current views are very close to those of Murray. While unemployment and labour market changes are still regarded as important, in an article for the *New Statesman* in early 1997 Field highlighted the role of divorce, family breakdown and illegitimacy as among the chief factors promoting the growth of an underclass, together with the spread of a 'lager lout' culture.[34] Implicitly there is an underlying stress on morality, duty and responsibilities. Again the similarities between Murray and Field are all too evident. Compare Murray's claim—'The long term welfare recipient...cannot feel self respect, no matter what is done on behalf of her dignity'[35]—with Field's: 'One of welfare's roles is to reward and to punish. The distribution of welfare is one of the great teaching forces open to advanced societies'.[36] All of which leads Field to conclude that 'welfare...should openly reward good behaviour and it should be used to enhance those roles which the country values'.[37]

Similar themes have also been taken up by Gordon Brown: 'Developing a welfare state built around the work ethic' is his self proclaimed primary objective.[38] It led to the establishment of a taskforce under the chief executive of Barclays Bank to modernise the taxation and benefits system, with the twin aims of combating welfare dependency and promoting work. As Brown said on the introduction of the Working Families Tax Credit, 'Work now pays—now go to work'.[39] At the same time 18 to 24 year olds who refuse subsidised work training or voluntary work were told their giros would be frozen for six months, prompting an unnamed Treasury source to argue, 'This is a real landmark in welfare reform... There will now be no excuse not to get a job'.[40]

Brown, Murray and Field are not alone in arguing that welfare undermines the 'character' of those in receipt of it. Such perspectives have been adopted by the Democrats in the US, and it is to the US that Field, Blair and other leading New Labour politicians have looked to find ways of 'thinking the unthinkable' about welfare. We have already noted that Clinton and his policy advisers have been influential in New Labour thinking. Labour has replaced the term 'social security' with 'welfare', which has more negative connotations in the US, and the US system of employment and welfare (including 'workfare' and 'tax credits') have been taken as a model in their discussions of social policy. In Clinton's 1992 election campaign there were commitments to good childcare provision, job creation and healthcare programmes. But central to his proposals was workfare.

While improvements in other areas of social policy have been ditched, workfare has continued apace in the US. In 1996 the Personal Responsibility and Work Opportunity Reconciliation Act was passed, which abolished universal entitlement to aid and introduced a five year limit of state support. Further, mothers aged 18 or below who were 'unwed', or children born to mothers under 18 who are already in receipt of aid, were in danger of having support cut or severely curtailed. As if that was not enough, all adult recipients were required to have secured some form of paid employment within two years of being on aid. With more than 30 million Americans living in poverty, the US has the highest proportion of poor people in the Western world, yet federal state welfare spending amounts to only 1 percent of the entire budget.[41] Proposed budget cuts in welfare spending in the US will see an additional 1 million children in poverty, and one ex-adviser to Clinton has estimated that without welfare nearly 58 million Americans would be officially poor.[42]

Central to New Labour's welfare reforms has been a call for the British population 'to work', and to those already in employment to work harder and more 'flexibly'. Importantly, work has become the key to solving problems of poverty, now termed social exclusion, and welfare dependency. For single parents, the young, the unemployed and other socially excluded groups, work is 'salvation' and the route to 'inclusion', to being part of Blair's modern Britain. Again this is couched in terms of individual responsibilities, not rights:

> *The responsibilities of individuals who can provide for themselves and their families to do so must always be matched by a responsibility on the part of government to provide opportunities for self advancement. The government's aim is to deliver services of such high quality that there would simply be no reason why people should not take them up... The government's commitment to expand significantly the range of help available therefore alters the contract with those who are capable of work. It is the government's responsibility to promote work opportunities and to help people take advantage of them. It is the responsibility of those who can take them up to do so... For example, the New Deal for Young People provides high quality options, all of which include education and training, designed to attract accredited qualifications. Those who unreasonably refuse an offer or fail to take up a place will be sanctioned.*[43]

Enforcing work commitments forms the basis of Labour's New Deal. Importantly the New Deal is not about creating jobs, but is once more about asserting a moral agenda: refashioning attitudes to work, creating a work ethic and stressing the importance of labour discipline. Work is, to use the terminology of New Labour, a matter of character, self respect, obligations and responsibilities. The problems facing many of Britain's growing numbers of the working poor are neglected here and will not be addressed through a low minimum wage.[44] From the autumn of 1999 there will be an even tighter regime of sanctions, with Brown claiming that 'there can be no excuse for staying at home on benefit and not taking jobs on offer'.[45]

Similarly the government has sought to continue with the Tory attempts to transform Britain into Europe's 'sweatshop'. Thus Mulgan claims that 'wellbeing is as much about life skills as it is about income',[46] while Field talks of the 'non-economic' causes of poverty. This desire for flexibility also provides a key to understanding Labour's coolness towards the trade unions, and its unwillingness to reverse the Tories' anti trade union legislation, whilst the minimum wage rate set at £3.60 an hour can only be understood as part of these wider, labour-cheapening goals.

Another key aspect of New Labour's welfare reforms is its concern to address social exclusion. For Mandelson, the biggest challenge which Labour faces is:

> ...*the growing number of our fellow citizens who lack the means, material and otherwise, to participate in economic, social, cultural and political life in Britain today. This is about more than poverty and unemployment. It is about being cut off from what the rest of us regard as normal life. It is called social exclusion, what others call the 'underclass'.*[47]

In the hands of New Labour social exclusion is used to replace any concern with inequality and redistribution. It is attractive because it moves the political goalposts from an emphasis upon structural causes of poverty and inequality to the individual's connections, or the absence of them, with paid forms of employment and to the 'community'. Income is not the issue. To quote Mandelson once more:

> *Let us be crystal clear on this point. The people we are concerned about, those in danger of dropping off the end of the ladder of opportunity and becoming disengaged from society, will not have their long term problems addressed by an extra pound a week on their benefits.*[48]

Blair launched the Social Exclusion Unit (SEU) in December 1997 under the slogan 'Bringing Britain Together'. The move was heralded by John Lloyd, *New Statesman* columnist and New Labour devotee, as 'an exposition of a revolution in the philosophy and practice of provision, in the conception of the welfare state, in the methods and ethos of addressing poverty'.[49] The unit was at the fore of Labour's efforts to develop a social policy underpinned by 'compassion with a hard edge'. Run by a former private secretary to John Major, the SEU is, according to Mandelson, modelled on the Tories' failed 'Action for the Cities' initiative, launched by Thatcher in 1987. In place of what are dismissed as Old Labour concerns with the standard of living and income levels of the poor, there is a focus upon Welfare to Work and the problems of inadequate parenting, school truancy, crime and delinquency, and those who sleep rough. With the SEU's Rough Sleeping Initiative announced in July 1998, for example, there was compulsion placed on those sleeping rough to take hostel accommodation once it was available. Those not doing this were warned that they may be forcibly removed from the streets. Similarly, where children truant or get involved in anti-social behaviour, the cause must be family breakdown or inadequacy and thus compulsory parenting classes become part of the solution. What we are witnessing is the pathologisation of the poor, where the hard edge of government policy is obvious but the compassion less apparent.

The stress on social exclusion marks Labour's abandonment of any wish to redistribute wealth and income and tackle the problems of increasing social polarisation. Several ministers have already stated that New Labour is not about equality of outcome, but equality of opportunity, with the emphasis on economic growth instead of redistribution.[50] As David Marquand, ex-SDP MP and now leading Blairite, puts it, New Labour is 'manifestly unshocked by the huge and growing disparities of income'.[51] Inherited wealth and income is regarded by Field simply as 'one of those unappreciated webs so binding families and friends together that individuals are knitted into society'.[52]

Labour has no anti-poverty policy as such, despite Darling's claim in August 1999 that Labour would 'free 1 million from poverty'.[53] Poverty is to be tackled through employment, the promotion of enterprise and an emphasis on duty and responsibility. For Mandelson and Roger Liddle, in their book *The Blair Revolution*, anti-poverty policy will be concerned with 'the irresponsible who fall down on their obligations to their families and therefore to their community'.[54]

Labour's abandonment of a commitment to redistribution, and its commitment to Tory tax policies, have been criticised from some very unexpected sources. Roy Hattersley has emerged as one of its strongest critics, dismissing not only the SEU but also attacking Gordon Brown's reluctance to address the issue of growing inequality. In a debate between them in the pages of *The Guardian* in the autumn of 1997,[55] Hattersley attacked Brown for New Labour's willingness to accept gross disparities in income and wealth, with Brown replying that equality of outcome simply imposed 'uniformity' and 'stifled human potential'.[56]

Labour has been a government of targets: a target for inflation, a target for borrowing levels, a target for interest rates, and both Blair and Darling have now announced a target for reducing poverty. But the prospects do not look good. Labour's refusal to address the real causes of poverty will lead to a growth in the numbers who are poor by 1 million between 1997 and 2002,[57] due in the main to rising levels of unemployment and the effects of Labour's own Welfare to Work and New Deal proposals.

This represents a damning indictment of New Labour and everything it stands for. Its leaders are willing to castigate and penalise the poor and disadvantaged, while at the same time promoting policies which increase their misery and hardship. Blair's desire to embrace the market and to extend the Tories' labour market and welfare policies will create unprecedented levels of affluence for the rich and big business but will do nothing to help the most needy and vulnerable. Blair and the Labour leadership claim their project is one which will create a new, modern and revitalised Britain: 'one nation' for the new millennium. The reality is very different. Britain is an increasingly divided country, divided between the rich and powerful on the one hand, and those who are poor and disadvantaged on the other. Indeed a government report published in September 1999 claims that Britain is fast becoming 'two nations' because of the divide between rich and poor.[58]

Blair's conservatism is also reflected in his adoption of the language of the new right: Labour's policy documents on welfare and poverty are permeated by the notions of welfare 'dependency', 'community', 'family', 'obligations', 'duties' and 'responsibilities'. Rights and entitlements to benefits, and decent schools, healthcare and housing hardly feature at all in this perspective. Further, the strong element of compulsion, enforcement and regulation in Blair's approach surpasses even that of the Tories. Labour's desire to attack benefit 'fraud' and welfare 'scroungers' has reached a new height. For Mandelson and Liddle 'New Labour's mission is to move forward from where Margaret Thatcher left off, rather than dismantling every single thing she did'.[59] In his speech to the 1997 Labour Party conference Blair argued that 'a decent society is not based on rights. It is based on duty. Our duty to each other. To all should be given opportunity; from all responsibility demanded.'

Despite all the talk of 'social-ism' and the 'Third Way', there is a pervasive conservatism at the heart of New Labour which forms the basis of Blair's much vaunted vision of a 'new society'. Blair talks of creating a 'new settlement' between the individual and society, wherein the stress on the individual will be accompanied by a new role for social institutions such as family, community and the state. At the forefront of this process is an attack on those on a range of benefits, but this is a wedge to drive a wider agenda of welfare restructuring where we all have the responsibility to provide for our pensions, our healthcare, the education of our children and so on. State provision is to be removed or, at the very least, residualised and stigmatised. This is an agenda to continue with the Tories' strategy of privatising what is left of the public sector and cutting the social wage. To emphasise the point, recent figures show that public spending is now at its lowest for 40 years, with even the Blairite *Guardian* claiming that 'Thatcher was more lavish than Labour'.[60]

Conclusion: New Labour in context

In part, New Labour's welfare agenda is a continuation of a number of themes that have been central to British government policy for the last

20 years—the attempt to reconstruct welfare and to establish a new welfare settlement. It is an attempt both to cut government spending and cheapen labour, to reinvigorate British capital and open up the British economy to multinational capital. But the project is also built around a deeply conservative moral agenda where the poor working class are increasingly identified as a problem who must be forced to accept the values of modern capitalism. For New Labour's ideologues the excluded must reintegrate themselves within modern society by engaging with work—in whatever conditions and for whatever rates of pay. For Blair and Co capitalism works and brings benefits to us all, but this necessitates us taking responsibility for our own welfare and not relying on the state, accepting that the world has changed and periods of unemployment are inevitable, and recognising that we are competing in a global labour market and thus need to work more flexibly and cheaply. For New Labour the state's role is reduced to one that enables citizens to provide their own welfare, but state provision is curtailed and focused on more disciplinary aspects of social control. Such commitments mean that even when there is an estimated surplus of up to £12 billion in the Treasury's 'war chest' the government will not voluntarily increase spending on wages or welfare.[61] This is an important point to emphasise. The war chest is not the result of a booming economy or a reduction in need but is a direct consequence of policy choices and the government's refusal to spend on much needed social and welfare services.

The problem for New Labour is that increasing numbers do not accept its logic. *Social Attitudes* surveys emphasise that we want more money spent on state welfare, that we want more trade union rights and better pay and working conditions. Further, whilst we are told to work harder for less, the bosses continue to award themselves huge salaries and perks. New Labour has tried to stigmatise and target different sections of the poor but its attacks on the disabled, pensioners, lone parents and refugees have provoked a response which has forced it to backtrack. In the months ahead there is little doubt that such attacks will continue and that they will continue to feed the hostility towards the Blair government within the labour movement—the degree to which New Labour will be successful is much less certain.

When we look at the New Labour government and its welfare policies there are two potential pitfalls to avoid. The first is to see them as something alien to the Labourist tradition and a complete break with anything Labour governments in the past could have done. The second danger is to see nothing new in New Labour: Labour always sells out; Blair is no different. While Labour governments have certainly always sold out, they were nevertheless ideologically committed to the politics of reformism, to dealing eventually with structural inequalities, to promoting equality of opportunity via comprehensive education and a national healthcare system, and to protecting, however inadequately, the poor by redistributing income. Within the ideology of New Labour, however, there clearly are a number of themes that break with traditional Labourist conceptions. New Labour's moralism, its rejection of the structural causes of poverty, acceptance of dramatic income inequality, attempts to pathologise the poor, and the promotion of a series of conservative family and community agendas, represents a substantial break with old Labourist ideology. The fact that Roy Hattersley has been such a trenchant critic of Blair and Brown perhaps emphasises the point. It is the enforcement of this new moralism that has created such disillusionment with the government from layers of old Labour and trade union activists and opened up an ideological struggle on the left over the politics, goals and strategies of socialist politics and the possibility of creating a better world.

Notes

1   'Blair Bounces Back But Should Tone Down The Moral Talk', *The Guardian*, 6 September 1999.
2   'Tearaways Banned From The Streets', *The Guardian*, 2 September 1999.
3   Tony Blair, quoted in the *Independent on Sunday*, 28 July 1996.
4   T Blair, *New Britain: My Vision of a Younger Country* (London, 1996), p59.
5   T Blair, *Ethics, Marxism and True Socialism*, Fabian Pamphlet 565 (London, 1994), p3.
6   Ibid, p5.
7   Tony Blair's speech to the 1996 Labour Party conference.
8   Quoted in *The Guardian*, 29 January 1996.
9   A Etzioni, *The Spirit of Community* (London, 1995), pix.
10 Quoted in A Callinicos, 'Betrayal and Discontent: Labour under Blair', *International Socialism* 72 (1996), p16.
11 M Rutter, H Giller and A Hagell, *Anti-Social Behavior by Young People* (Cambridge, 1998), p66.
12 Ibid, p1.
13 Quoted in C Jones and T Novak, *Poverty, Welfare and the Disciplinary State* (London, 1999), p5.
14 See report on the Hamilton curfew in *Socialist Worker*, 29 August 1998.
15 'Blair's Moral Crusade', *The Observer*, 5 September 1999.
16 Jack Straw, quoted in *The Guardian*, 15 October 1996, p2.
17 Secretary of State for Social Security and Minister for Welfare Reform, *New Ambitions for Our Country: A New Contract for Welfare* (London, 1988), pp13, 57, 59.
18 'Labour Targets Lazy Parents', *The Guardian*, 16 January 1998.
19 'Nationwide Network Planned For Lessons In Parenting', *The Guardian*, 24 July 1998.
20 C Harman, 'Globalisation: a Critique of a New Orthodoxy', *International Socialism* 73 (Winter 1996).
21 A Giddens, 'Beyond Left and Right', *The Observer*, 13 September 1998, p27.
22 T Blair, *New Britain...*, op cit, p121.
23 A Giddens, 'After The Left's Paralysis', *New Statesman*, 1 May 1998, p18.

24   In the language of the green paper on public health ('Our Healthier Nation'), 'individual victim blaming' and 'nanny state engineering'.

25   R Cook, 'A Radical Agenda for a New Millennium', *Renewal*, vol 5, no 1 (1997), p10.

26   See C Harman, 'Globalisation: a Critique of a New Orthodoxy', op cit, and A Rogers, 'Is There A New "Underclass"?', *International Socialism* 40 (Autumn 1988) for a critique of many of the ideas behind such claims.

27   T Blair, Foreword and Introduction, in Secretary of State for Social Security and Minister for Welfare Reform, op cit.

28   Commission on Social Justice, *Social Justice: Strategies for National Renewal* (London, 1994), pp1, 224.

29   H Glennerster and J Hills (eds), *The State of Welfare*, 2nd edn (Oxford, 1998). See also summary report by authors in *The Guardian*, 22 April 1998.

30   When he was not preaching to the poor and condemning 'welfare cheats' and 'Jack the lads', to use his terms, he was busy witch hunting socialists from Birkenhead Labour Party during the 1980s.

31   Field's publications for the IEA include: *Stakeholder Welfare* (London, 1996); (with L M Mead) *From Welfare to Work* (London, 1997); and a contribution to *Charles Murray and the Underclass: The Developing Debate* (London, 1996).

32   See C Murray, *The Emerging British Underclass* (London, 1990), and *Underclass: The Crisis Deepens* (London, 1994); and IEA, *Charles Murray and the Underclass*, op cit.

33   F Field, *Losing Out: The Emergence of Britain's Underclass* (London, 1989).

34   F Field, 'The Underclass Of 97', *New Statesman*, 17 January 1997, p30.

35   C Murray, *In Pursuit of Happiness and Good Government* (New York, 1988), p130.

36   F Field, *Stakeholder Welfare*, op cit, p111.

37   C Jones and T Novak, op cit, p15.

38   Quoted in *The Observer*, 11 May 1997.

39   'Go To Work Or I'll Freeze Your Giro, Warns Brown', *The Observer*, 5 September 1999.

40   Ibid.

41   R Link, 'Beware Echoes Of Disraeli: Welfare Policies Tell The World That In The USA It Is A Sin To Be Poor', *Poverty*, no 97 (Summer 1997), p12.

42   Ibid, p14.

43   Secretary of State for Social Security and Minister for Welfare Reform, op cit, p31.

44   If we adopt the Council of Europe's 'Decency Threshold', which classifies all workers earning below two thirds of the average wage as poor, 48 percent of workers in Britain are poor.

45   'Brown Takes On The Jobless', *The Herald*, 6 September 1999.

46   G Mulgan, 'Think Wellbeing, Not Welfare', *New Statesman*, 17 January 1997, p28.

47   P Mandelson, *Labour's Next Steps: Tackling Social Exclusion* (London, 1997), p1.

48   Ibid, p7.

49   J Lloyd, quoted in the *New Statesman*, 29 August 1997.

50   C Smith, *New Questions for Socialism* (London, 1996), p5.

51   D Marquand, 'The Blair Paradox', *Prospect*, May 1998, p18.

52   F Field, *Stakeholder Welfare*, op cit, p42.

53   'We'll Get Rid Of The Poor', *The Observer*, 22 August 1999.

54   P Mandelson and R Liddle, *The Blair Revolution* (London, 1996), p20.

55   See *The Guardian*, 26 July, 6 August and 21 August 1997

56 During its 1997 conference week Labour was also criticised by 54 of Britain's leading social policy academics who, in a letter to the *Financial Times*, called for redistribution, a move which cut little ice with Blair and Brown.

57 D Piachaud, 'The Prospects for Poverty', *New Economy*, March 1988, p12.

58 'Shock For Blair Over "Two-Nation Britain" ', *The Independent*, 8 September 1999.

59 Ibid.

60 'Public Spending Lowest For 40 Years', *The Guardian*, 25 August 1999.

61 'Labour Heads For £12bn War Chest', *The Guardian*, 17 September 1999.

Benign imperialism versus United Nations

KEN COATES

'Sovereignty is less absolute than in earlier times. Just as we now consider it right to intervene in families to prevent domestic violence, so it
has become normal to override state sovereignty in cases of large scale
violations of human rights'.[1] This is the rationale proposed by Mary
Kaldor to justify NATO's decision to bomb Yugoslavia. Ever since the
Cold War ended, she claims, 'the distinction between internal peace and
external war, between a domestic rule of law and international anarchy
that characterised the Westphalian era has broken down'.[2] Indeed, she
continues, since the Second World War 'there has been steady progress
towards a global legal regime which deals both with the laws of war and
with human rights, and which has been strengthened by bodies like
Amnesty.'

And so we arrive at a new role for the North Atlantic Treaty
Organisation: 'benign or ethical imperialism'. NATO at 50 must 'switch
from defence of the West to upholding international law everywhere'.
There are some pretty serious difficulties about all this. Firstly, there is
not so much international law as Ms Kaldor believes. If the upholding of
human rights were to legitimate intervention, then larger transgressions
should mean brisker responses: but the truth is very far from this. More,
a large part of the responsibility for the failure to generate such rights
based law falls on the leader of NATO, the US. It is the US which repeatedly refused to ratify the Convention on Genocide,[3] until it gave way
with the reservation that, before any dispute to which the United States is

a party may be submitted to the jurisdiction of the court, 'the specific consent of the US is required in each case'. It is the US which refused to recognise the competence of the International Court of Justice in The Hague in the case of Nicaragua, and which defied 15 specific judgements condemning the actions of the US government and awarding compensation to the Nicaraguan government. It is the US which is the largest defaulter on its financial payments to the United Nations.

In all these cases, senior American politicians have claimed that UN decisions must be set aside if they conflict with the interest of the US government. Admittedly, the American state is the most powerful at large in today's world, so that when it stands off from the principles of international order as agreed by all the other states, by that fact alone it goes a long way to neutralise such principles. Noam Chomsky gives us a much better guide to the real legal position. There is, he says, a regime of international law and order, based on the United Nations Charter, and on the resolutions of the United Nations, together with the decisions of the World Court. This regime rests on the doctrines of national sovereignty, and outlaws the use of force, or even the threat of force between states, unless this has the express authority of the security council. In parallel, there is a Universal Declaration of Human Rights which guarantees the rights of individuals against states, but which provides no legal mechanism for upholding such guarantees and offers no guidance on how the UN Charter can be amended or suspended to provide for its enforcement. To be lawful, any attempt to reconcile this contradiction would need to be based upon consensus. Conquest could impose a solution to the problem, but would itself be unlawful under this system.

'Benign imperialisms' could only make law if they conquered everyone and then proclaimed a new law. Even the potent US might balk at this task, which would involve the generation of active government on a forbidding scale. It would surely militarise the economy and thus be inimical to the freedom of enterprise, or at any rate market sovereignty. Short of such highly improbable conquest, consensus is the only way to international law.

Ms Kaldor thinks that we can derive a formula that will help us from Immanuel Kant. She is right that Kant can help us, but he will offer no support whatever to benign imperialism. His proposal was to secure perpetual peace among states, and so, unsurprisingly, like the United Nations organisation, he considered states to be the foundation of the international order. A state is a society of human beings, Kant tells us, that no one other than itself can command or dispose of. Regarding conquest, of which he disapproves, Kant has a simple remedy: standing armies should be abolished. Kant's fifth principle is that 'no state shall forcibly interfere in the constitution and government of another state.'

The right to perpetual peace, then, will depend upon reforming states in such a manner as to provide them all with 'republican' or constitutional governments. Once they became similar, or sufficiently alike, they could then embrace federalism in a League of Nations which 'need not be a state of nations'. In this, as in other matters, Kant's essay is prescient, and its echoes are still resounding.

Certainly the present United Nations has not evolved sufficient congruities among its members to induce them voluntarily to accept such federalism, which might indeed provide for the agreement of enforceable human rights. The question does not arise, although the problem can clearly be seen. The enforcement of human rights today depends, as much as it ever has, on the development of public opinion, both within states and between them.

This was the foundation upon which we tried to build the Russell Tribunals which investigated the abuse of human rights, first of all in relation to torture and violent oppression in Latin America, and later considering other abuses, such as the mistreatment of indigenous peoples. In a number of sessions, key witnesses were interrogated, and the evidence of abuse was evaluated. The findings of the tribunals were widely reported in the press. The tribunals became necessary because, in the words of Lelio Basso, 'human rights are at the same time proclaimed and left unprotected, devoid of international or national safeguards'. But when Basso gave his authority to upholding human rights in Latin America in the 1970s, the science of spin was in its infancy. Today public opinion is almost a department of state, so that it becomes ever more difficult even to imagine what justice might be. Mary Kaldor is right to say that the work of Amnesty International has powerfully assisted in the creation of a public opinion which now both sustains and feeds on a wide variety of more specialised human rights agencies.

But, without the reform of the international system, there is no law to justify the intervention of any state or group of states, or to support the use of force to uphold human rights in any other state. Ms Kaldor implies that humanitarian intervention is a matter of opportunity because, although there are many cases in which it is not possible, 'that is not a reason to stand aside' when it is possible. The condition thus described has nothing whatever to do with law. It would fit, perhaps, the primitive rules which guarantee circumscribed security in gangland. Certain types of crimes will be punished if they simultaneously offend one or other of the principal gangsters. Other victims of arbitrary misbehaviour need not apply for such 'justice'. But law gives equal treatment to all cases, so all victims are entitled to equal redress. Discriminatory treatment is the antithesis of law.

Numerous commentators have compared the repression in Kosovo before the US bombardment with the sustained and ferocious military action of the Turkish state against the Kurds in south east Turkey. In fact, repressive legislation against the Kosovans had rightly aroused sustained opposition elsewhere in Europe since 1989,[4] but it was nothing like as bad as the more comprehensive repression, indeed slaughter, of Kurds in Turkey. As repression fomented rebellion, massacres became more common and more bloody. And yet Kaldor's benign imperialism recruits one set of oppressors from Turkey, under the flag of NATO, in order to redress the complaints of another set of oppressed in Kosovo. Justice would require that an impartial hearing be granted to both Kosovans and Kurds, and their separate complaints adjudicated within the framework of even handed fidelity to the law. If it is possible to bomb Belgrade in pursuit of justice, it is equally possible to bomb Ankara. The logistics involved are not the problem. The problem is that the bombardment of our Turkish ally is as unthinkable to NATO, as is justice for the Kurds. The Turkish establishment are our own oppressors, and it is necessary to be evil minded to see any equivalence at all between their behaviour and that alleged against Yugoslav Serbs.

Of course, in reality, bombing from outside is no more conducive to the defence of human rights in Kurdistan than it was in Kosovo: in both cases the remedy was or would be even worse than the original disorder. But we are not engaged in a plea for benign imperialism. It is not necessary to list the fearful roster of gross violations of human rights around the world to see that the only pretexts for intervention which concern benevolent imperialism are those in which some material strategic concern already exists. But the law does need to be reformed, because proxy wars, destabilisation and direct manipulation are more and more common in the modern world, and indeed are frequently found to be happening under the tutelage of the US or other NATO allies.

Until comparatively recently the European allies would quite normally have sought diplomatic release from the more bellicose US projects by a very simple device. They would have brought in an appeal to the UN in order to find a diplomatically acceptable way of getting out of the unwanted Yugoslav confrontations. Why did they not do this in the case of Yugoslavia? They could then have relied on Russia or China to veto the bombardment and thus escaped the responsibility for blocking the US project themselves. But by arranging to bypass the security council and its veto, the European allies have achieved a number of very undesirable results, most of which damage them far more than their possible adversaries.

Firstly, they have given the US hegemony over some important future decisions in the Balkans and further afield, which they are likely to find rather embarrassing and quite difficult to modify. Secondly, by breaching the rule of unanimity among the Great Powers represented by the veto, they have not secured any better mechanism for avoiding serious collisions of interest. The US and China can come into fierce conflict, and the possible beginnings of this can already be seen in Taiwan and even Kashmir. The veto was a poor instrument for the maintenance of peace, and no doubt it would be possible to improve on it. But to kick it away before any alternative has been devised will not be deemed very sensible by future generations.

China will presumably veto any 'humanitarian intervention', because it will not wish to welcome such an intervention into Tibet or Xinjiang. At this time, though, there is not much likelihood of Ms Kaldor's freedom legions following her up the Himalayas. The Dalai Lama thinks that public opinion can still play an important part in moderating China's behaviour in Tibet. Certainly he understands the limits of benign imperialism. During the Gulf War, after I had conducted hearings with him in the European Parliament, I wrote to him to ask if he could support the pope's stance on that conflict. He replied by saying that there were undoubtedly some similarities between the cases of Kuwait and Tibet, 'but unfortunately, so far as is known, in Tibet there is absolutely no oil whatever to be found.' Perhaps that reinforces his view that, in Tibet's case, the movement of argument and persuasion is more likely to be effective than military action of any kind.

But, yes, there needs to be a continuous effort to create a more civilised international regime, in which human rights may genuinely flourish. This needs to be a regime of law, and it is difficult to see how any progress towards this can be made by destroying the frail system that was created at the end of the Second World War. Back in 1945 destruction had raged across the world and focused the minds of governments everywhere. The impulse to avoid new wars was powerful enough to give us the UN Charter, with all its faults and all its promises. Nobody can expect governments to suddenly improve and be made moral by their agreement to league together in a United Nations. But they are not worsened in this effort either.

The problem which has been created by the actions of benign or ethical imperialism is, of course, that it has seriously undermined the UN. That the most powerful state can lead its allies into a unilateral military onslaught, without the express endorsement of the security council, means that brute force alone now determines whether any other state or combination of states might take unilateral action in their own interests. Conflict zones abound around the world, and most of them engender fairly serious cases of human rights abuse. Ethical imperialism is supposed to sound quite innocuous. But what if there were to be several such imperialisms?

It is not likely that the UN machinery will disintegrate as a result of the war in the Balkans. But it has been undermined, and it may begin to give way to other alliances, calculated to ward off the hegemony of US ethics. The true face of these ethics was revealed by Mr Karl Bildt, speaking for the UN in a television interview on *Newsnight* on 28 July 1999, about the progress made in organising international aid for the reconstruction of those areas of Yugoslavia, including Kosovo, which had been devastated during the war. Mr Bildt maintained that it was difficult, if not impossible, to aid Serbia, because the economic system there was not conducive to receiving aid. That is how far the sovereignty of the market place has undermined that of ethics. Yugoslavia had established a form of market socialism with self management, which functioned adequately. But was it this unusual economic system as modified by the IMF, rather than any ethical judgements on its leaders and administrators, which informed Mr Bildt's response to questioners? Or was it the war economy of Yugoslavia which could not be aided?

If ethical imperialism is driven by the need to assert the absolute domination of market forces over society, there will be other states which begin to find it tiresome. And the UN will have to contend with the ideological debates which ensue. In short, the Balkan War has established a new order of extreme instability and insecurity. That is why the parliament of the Ukraine voted recently for nuclear rearmament, because it felt that the security guarantees it had previously been given by the US were no longer valid. That is why the Russian government, caught in a very precarious political balance, encouraged statements to the effect that it was now abandoning its 'no first use' pledge. Ethical imperialism has thus begun the reversal of all the gains which had previously been made to limit and control the possibilities of nuclear war.

The ink on this article was scarcely dry when all the issues which it discusses were highlighted once again, in the savage tragedy of East Timor. East Timor was a classic victim of old imperialisms, which never pretended to be benign. The former colonial power, Portugal, was by far the most humane actor involved, however. The 1975 invasion by Indonesia was unbelievably brutal and murderous. The Western allies encouraged it. There is evidence that the US actively approved of it, and the British continued to supply a comprehensive range of armaments before, during and after the East Timor bloodbath, in which Indonesian forces killed more than 200,000 people.

The recent revolutionary upheaval in Indonesia, following economic collapse, loosened the grip of the Indonesian state on its East Timorese colony and produced an agreement for a referendum on independence. Now that the result of the referendum has been as decisive as everyone expected, the Indonesian military are determined to prevent its implementation, and another terrible bloodbath is already beginning. But there is no benign or ethical face on the global imperialism which confronts this dreadful situation. Neither the US nor its British dogs of war are in the least bit moved to intervention by the worst human rights violations in the modern world.

The intervention in Kosovo showed how heartlessly great military power could be used. But the non-intervention in East Timor shows that it can be even more heartlessly not used.

Notes

1 *The Observer*, 18 July 1999.
2 'A Benign Imperialism', *Prospect*, April 1999.
3 This convention was unanimously adopted by the UN General Assembly in 1948, and came into force in January 1951. It was signed by the US but not ratified by the Senate, on the grounds that it was poorly drafted and could allow intervention by other governments in US affairs. The Senate again refused to ratify in 1984, while supporting the 'principles embodied in the convention'. It was finally ratified on 25 November 1988, with the reservation.
4 In the early 1990s I received Ibrahim Rugova and a group of leading Kosovans as chairman of the Sub-committee on Human Rights in the European Parliament. Although we obtained a sympathetic response from our colleagues, I cannot say that much was done to help redress the grievances of which Rugova was complaining.

Is the UN an alternative to 'humanitarian imperialism'?

JOHN BAXTER

In the recent Balkan War we have seen the concept of humanitarian intervention used to justify the massive military onslaught against Serbia. Robin Cook was particularly keen to justify the bombings. He declared the intervention to be a 'war against fascism'. He compared the regime to that of fascist Spain in the 1930s and demanded that the left rally to his cause.[1] Many on the left, including Ken Livingstone, did back the slaughter.

The concept of 'humanitarian war' is not entirely new. We should remember that in scores of previous wars our rulers have attempted to justify themselves by reference to the justice of their cause and the evil of the enemy.[2] Nevertheless, a new generation of liberal thinkers have been swayed by the rhetoric used to justify recent wars. Mary Kaldor, the proponent of humanitarian intervention criticised by Ken Coates in his article, is a case in point. She was perhaps best known as a prominent member of European Nuclear Disarmament, contributing with Ken and others to E P Thompson's collection of essays in favour of nuclear disarmament, *Protest and Survive*.[3] Her transition from peace activist in the early 1980s to enthusiast for military intervention in the 1990s began with her calls for military intervention in Bosnia.[4] In her article in *The Observer* she argues that the world is entering a new era where, as a result of global interdependence, 'wars between states...are becoming an anachronism.' Instead 'the new wars such as those in Bosnia, Kosovo or Rwanda are waged against civilians, and are fought in the name of ethnically exclusive claims to power'.[5]

But while Kaldor welcomes the precedent set in Kosovo, she doesn't like the form that this humanitarian intervention actually took. Against the horrors of actually existing humanitarian intervention she holds up an ideal whose political goal 'is to support democrats rather than to negotiate from above with the warring parties', and which 'is defensive and non-escalatory by definition'.[6] This all rather smacks of second thoughts—after all, as early as January 1999 Kaldor was calling for the use of ground troops and the extension of the area of operation of UN forces to 'confine local military forces to their compounds'.[7] Later, when the intervention was launched under NATO auspices, she argued that bombing could only be justified if rapidly followed by deployment of ground troops.[8] Today, with the ethnic cleansing of Kosovan Serbs taking place with the connivance of Western forces, and the devastation of the bombing, Kaldor can only keep hold of her liberal conscience by arguing that this is not what she meant by humanitarian intervention!

Ken Coates is absolutely right to attack the muddled thinking and apologetics for imperialism that underlie Kaldor's arguments. He rightly points out the double standard of supporting Western intervention, supposedly to defend human rights and stop transgressions of international law in Iraq and Kosovo, whilst ignoring repression at the hands of Western allies. When Ken argues that 'against ethical imperialists there needs to be a new peace movement', he is absolutely correct, but in order to be able to build such a movement we need to be clear who our friends and enemies are. In this article I would like to take up Ken's argument that in order to 'create a more civilised international regime, in which human rights may flourish' we have to reform the United Nations.[9] This article will focus on the differences in our analysis, but it should be stressed from the outset that this discussion is only meant to further aims which we both hold.

'The impulse to avoid new wars'?

Ken argues that, at the end of the Second World War, 'the impulse to avoid new wars was powerful enough to give us the UN Charter, with all its faults and all its promises.' It is true that the Charter, signed in San Francisco in 1945 by the founding states of the UN, is a statement ringing with hope for all humanity. It resolved:

> *...to save succeeding generations from the scourge of war, which twice in our lifetime has brought untold sorrow to mankind, to reaffirm faith in human rights, in the dignity and worth of the human person, in the equal rights of men and women and of nations large and small, to establish conditions under which justice and respect for the obligations arising from treaties and other*

sources of international law can be maintained, to promote social progress and better standards of life in larger freedom.[10]

But, given the last 54 years of repeated wars, oppression and abuses of human rights, we would have to conclude that the UN has failed in its task. The question that we have to answer is whether this failure arises from something fundamental to the UN, or whether it is an organisation we could hope to change. Many on the left, including those like Ken who stood out against the bombing of the former Yugoslavia, will agree that the UN has its faults, but argue that the principles of the UN Charter are an ideal worth fighting for, and that we must fight for its reform. For many, the experience of the war over Kosovo reinforced this idea. After all, the US and its allies by-passed the UN in order to avoid Russian and Chinese vetoes on the Security Council.

However, it is wrong to mistake the laudable rhetoric which so often emerges from the UN for its real purpose. The UN did not emerge out of people's hopes for peace, but from the machinations of the Great Powers as they existed at the close of the war. The fact that in Kosovo the UN did not prove useful for the US and its allies should not distract us. The UN is, and always has been, the creature of the major imperialist powers. For the last 50 years the US has been the most powerful imperialist nation, and as such it has been the US that has dominated the organisation.

The birth of the United Nations

The UN was launched in 1945 at the close of the Second World War. Officials within the US State Department had been planning for peace from as early as 1941, and by 1943 the formation of the United Nations was a declared objective of US foreign policy.[11] The closing years of the war saw rounds of conferences at Tehran, Yalta and Potsdam as the three major powers, the US, Russia and Britain, horse-traded for influence. The launch of the United Nations was part of this process.

The shifting alliances and splits between and within the ruling classes of the different countries founding the UN were complex, but, put simply, Russia and Britain saw their interests as being to maintain the pre-war system of spheres of interest, acting as largely independent trading blocs. For Britain this reflected the desire to hold on to empire and to develop a trading block in Western Europe. For Russia it reflected the desire to develop a sphere of influence in Eastern Europe.[12] Russia and Britain were lukewarm about the prospect of the United Nations but were not prepared to openly oppose it.

The US emerged from the war the most powerful nation, with more than half of the world's industrial capacity, almost two thirds of the world's gold reserves and a military capacity which dwarfed that of other states.[13] The desire to prevent damaging wars was no doubt important to US strategists, but only in so far as wars damaged American interests. Those interests were reflected in a desire to see free trade throughout the world, so as to provide open access for America's powerful business interests. The creation of the United Nations would provide a forum in which the US could use its weight to hold back the aspirations of its former allies to create trading blocks resistant to American influence.[14] But at the same time the US wanted to maintain and develop its own sphere of influence in South America and the Pacific. In the words of John McCloy, US Assistant Secretary of War at the time, 'We ought to be able to have our cake and eat it too...we ought to be free to operate under this regional arrangement in South America, and at the same time intervene promptly in Europe'.[15]

Whilst at times the US had to make compromises in order to keep the Allies on board, it was always American interests which dominated in the negotiations to set up the UN. What emerged from the negotiations was a United Nations system dominated by the Security Council, which was in turn controlled by the five permanent members. The five represent the balance of power as it existed at the close of the war: the three Allies, with France and China.

At the launch of the UN, as today, other countries had to be satisfied with membership of the General Assembly, a talking shop which has passed thousands of resolutions but has no real power. Even so, at the founding of the UN, America wanted to ensure that the Assembly would not pass any embarrassing resolutions, and made sure it was packed with powers sympathetic to the US. The criterion for membership was a declaration of war on the Axis Powers. The US pressured its previously neutral allies in South America to declare war by the deadline of 1 March 1945. The success of this strategy can be judged from the fact that in the first seven years of the General Assembly (1946-1953) of the 800 resolutions adopted the US was defeated in less than 3 percent, and in no case were important US security interests involved.[16]

The UN during the Cold War: 1945-1989

Within two years of the founding of the UN the Cold War had begun. A terrible symmetry was imposed on the world, with the two Great Powers armed to the teeth with nuclear weapons. Whilst there was no conflict at the heart of the system, the two superpowers fought their wars largely by proxy at the edges of the system. Between 1945 and 1989 there were 138 wars, resulting in 23 million deaths. All were fought in the so called Third World. The Korean War killed 3 million, the Vietnam War 2 million. Military interventions not classified as wars, like those in

Hungary in 1956, Czechoslovakia in 1968 and Grenada in 1983, claimed thousands of lives.[17]

The US attitude to the UN General Assembly changed during this period. In the early years when it could count on a majority in the Assembly it was particularly keen on using the Assembly to promote its initiatives and, if necessary, to bypass the Security Council. However, during the 1960s, as decolonisation gathered pace, a seat in the General Assembly was seen as a confirmation of nationhood, and the number of members soared. By 1961 the numbers had grown from 51 to 100, and by 1993 there were 184.[18] America's dominance was destroyed. On more than one occasion the Assembly has condemned US actions, for example in 1983 when it described the invasion of Grenada as 'a flagrant violation of international law'.[19] The difficulty in controlling the Assembly votes forced an uneasy alliance between the USSR and America to re-establish the role of the Security Council, and since 1961 all UN military action has been authorised by the Council.[20] This recalcitrance on the part of the Assembly also explains why in the mid-1980s both countries were unwilling to pay their full financial contributions to the UN, leading to a crisis in funding.[21]

The period of the Cold War is recognised by even the most sympathetic liberal commentators as a period in which the standoff between America and the USSR prevented the UN from acting as an effective peacekeeper.[22] In the major conflicts (with the exception of Korea) the UN stood back and let the superpowers get on with it. The US and the USSR could slaughter with impunity in Vietnam, Hungary, Czechoslovakia, Afghanistan and Cambodia, sometimes monitored by UN observers. The other permanent members did not tend to involve themselves in conflicts where their interests could clash with those of America. On the one occasion when France and Britain did, in Suez in 1956, America was able to bypass their vetoes on the Security Council and push a motion through the General Assembly calling for their withdrawal. Britain and France had to bow to their economically superior ally.[23] But where the US had no interests, the other permanent members could intervene without fear of interference from the UN: France was able to launch brutal wars to defend its colonies in Algeria and Indochina; China invaded Tibet; Britain murdered and tortured thousands to crush the so called Mau Mau rebellion in Kenya in 1953. Countries outside of the Security Council elite have also been able to get away with slaughter when it has not been in the interests of the Great Powers to intervene. The UN did nothing when Indonesia took advantage of the withdrawal of Portuguese troops from East Timor in 1975, launching an invasion in which over 200,000 were killed.

The UN after the Cold War

For many the end of the Cold War seemed to offer the possibility that the UN-could finally act as a force for peace.[24] With the end of the Cold War we have certainly entered a new era of international relations, but any hope that the UN would come into its own has been demolished by the experience of the last ten years. The US has not sought collaboration, but instead has sought to take advantage of the weakness of its main rival and attempted to construct a New World Order in its own image. In the early 1990s it appeared that the UN could become the plaything of American strategic interests, but as the decade has dragged on it has become increasingly difficult for the US to use the UN to sanction its military operations. It has chosen instead to develop the role of NATO.[25] However, that is not to say that the UN is no longer useful to America in some circumstances, or to predict its imminent demise.

Iraq

The UN-sanctioned war against Iraq showed exactly the form that post Cold War co-operation could take. Russia's weakness after the revolutions of 1989, its desire to secure US investment, and its own strategic interests in the region meant it was prepared to give its backing to the Gulf War. China too was anxious to develop trade links with the US and abstained when, on 30 November 1990, the Security Council passed a resolution sanctioning the use of military force. Within weeks Russia was repaid when Bush authorised the shipment of $1 billion worth of food to the USSR, while the ban on high level US-Chinese meetings, imposed after Tiananmen Square, was lifted.[26] The war was launched in January 1991.[27]

The reason given for launching the second Gulf War was that Iraq had broken international law by invading a sovereign country, Kuwait. In fact, Saddam Hussein had every reason to think he could resolve his border dispute with Kuwait by military means. The UN had said nothing when Iraq invaded the sovereign state of Iran in 1980, launching the Iran-Iraq war, which would last eight years. It suited US and Soviet interests to see Iran and Iraq tied up in a war of attrition.[28] It was only after seven years of slaughter, when it appeared that Iran might win the war, that the Security Council finally determined that there had been a breach of the peace between the two countries.[29] America could not afford to see its arch-enemy in the region strengthened by victory, and so joined the war on the side of Iraq. The intervention was the key to changing the balance of forces and gave Iraq its victory.

The fact that Hussein murdered and tortured his opponents didn't matter when he was fighting the Ayatollah Khomeini. However, when the monster the US had created got out of hand, Hussein was branded the 'new Hitler' to justify the onslaught against Iraq. This too was a 'humanitarian intervention', a war against fascism. Then, too, the humanitarian rhetoric won converts amongst the liberal left.[30] In reality, the war was necessary for two related reasons. The first was that the US was not prepared to see a huge proportion of world's oil reserves fall under Hussein's control.[31] The related strategic reason was that America was determined to construct its New World Order, to stamp US authority on the world and to banish forever the spectre of the Vietnam syndrome. The horrors of the Gulf War were conducted under the UN flag and this war against the Iraqi people continues to this day. Almost every day British and US jets continue to bomb targets in Iraq. UN sanctions are still killing 6,000 infants every month, and 2 million have died since the sanctions were imposed.[32]

Somalia

After America's relatively easy triumph under a UN flag in the Gulf, US president Bush was eager to reinforce his New World Order with another show of military might. The unfortunate country Bush chose was Somalia. Somalia was riven by warring factions and clans. These had grown originally out of the colonial exploits of the British, Italian and French states in the late 19th century, and had been revived as a result of various Cold War interventions. In December 1992 the UN launched 'Operation Restore Hope', again claiming to be launching a 'humanitarian intervention'.[33] Relations between the US and Russia were still good and the relevant motion was passed unanimously in the Security Council.[34] American and UN troops were sent in huge numbers with a mandate to keep the warring factions apart and to allow food and other relief to reach the dying people. The Bush administration, then in its last days, claimed that 2 million people would be saved from certain starvation and death. In fact, while one optimistic report suggested that between 10,000 and 25,000 lives may have been saved,[35] US troops alone claimed 10,000 casualties in a six month period in 1993.[36]

Far from keeping the peace and maintaining any pretence of neutrality, the US veered between cosying up to one faction and then to another, unsure as to who could provide the safest ally. It initially looked to the leader of the Somali National Alliance, General Aidid (the US Special Envoy even rented his house from one of Aidid's senior aides). Yet US troops sat back and did nothing when one particularly vicious group overran the city of Kismayo, kicking out Aidid's forces. This contrasts to their response to the crowds who demonstrated in Mogadishu to protest at the lack of action, many of whom were shot and killed by UN peacekeepers. Later, when Aidid proved an unreliable ally, US forces bombed a block of flats where civilian supporters of Aidid were holding a meeting, killing untold numbers of innocent people. They rained shells and missiles on a Mogadishu hospital where they thought he might be hiding, killing patients and staff.[37]

UN troops from all over the world committed atrocities against Somali civilians. Internal UN documents openly referred to Somali civilians as the enemy. Pictures appeared in the world's press showed Belgian troops roasting a Somali boy over a fire. The troops involved were brought to trial but were acquitted because the Somali child had never brought a complaint. When an American Gunnery Sergeant shot a boy dead for allegedly trying to steal his sunglasses, his punishment was the loss of one month's pay and demotion. Italian troops looted refugee camps. Malaysians beat up hospital staff. Pakistanis and Nigerians shot unarmed protesters.[38]

The American-led UN intervention was a disaster. The experience has been aptly summarised by Alex de Waal:

> *Operation Restore Hope was launched in December 1992 amid shocking— and carefully orchestrated—images of anarchy and starvation in Somalia, with the mandate of 'creating a secure environment for the delivery of humanitarian relief'. Eight months later it turned into the greatest US military humiliation since Vietnam. In three months of urban counter-guerrilla warfare against the unpaid, irregular but resourceful militia of General Mohamed Farah Aidid in Mogadishu City, US military doctrines of overwhelming force and near-zero American casualties came unstuck. The culmination was the 3 October battle, after which pictures of a dead US pilot being dragged through the streets by a jeering crowd and the plight of another taken prisoner of war... forced a truce and US withdrawal.*[39]

Relief charities like CARE-US, USAID and OXFAM-US were amongst the first to call for troops. Their demand was that UN troops should be there to protect the aid workers. In practice this meant that the lives of ordinary Somalis were of secondary importance.[40]

Rwanda

If Somalia was a disaster, words cannot express the scale of the UN's failure in Rwanda. The term 'genocide' has been frequently misused in relation to the situation in the former Yugoslavia, but no other word will do to describe the slaughter in Rwanda which left one in ten of the population dead.[41]

The killings were almost universally described as the result of ethnic tensions, but the troubles can be directly traced to the impact of imperialism on Rwanda. Before the arrival of European colonialism, the distinction between Hutus and Tutsis, the two major ethnic groups, was related to their economic role. The arrival of German and later Belgian colonialists cemented these divisions.[42] Using the classical divide and rule strategy of European colonialists, the Belgians used the Tutsi elite as an local ruling class. However, during decolonisation in the 1950s the Tutsi ruling class was in favour of a rapid withdrawal of the Belgians, seeing this as the only way they could hope to resist the demands for Hutu majority rule. Belgium saw the demands for national liberation from the Tutsi elite as dangerous and Communist-inspired and hoped to curry favour with the Hutu elite, who were in favour of a slower withdrawal so that they could build their own power base. Belgian troops fought side by side with Hutu militias in order to oust the Tutsi rulers in the so called 1959 revolution.[43] The new Hutu ruling class consolidated its position by playing the ethnic card.

The current period of crisis began with the massive fluctuations in coffee and tin prices in the late 1980s, and the IMF and World Bank's structural adjustment programme in 1989-1990 which saw the government's budget slashed by almost half. In order to distract attention from the attacks on the living standards of Hutu peasants, the government turned to scapegoating the Tutsis. At the same time the Rwandese Patriotic Front (RPF), an organisation based on Tutsi refugees, was launching attacks from its bases in Uganda.

The reason for outlining the lead up to the slaughter in such detail is in order to give the lie to the simplistic assumptions of Kaldor, who classifies the war as one of the new type, 'waged against civilians…in the name of ethnically exclusive claims to power'. To dismiss the events in Rwanda as arising simply from differences in ethnicity is to ignore both the complicity of Western institutions like the World Bank and IMF, and the legacy of colonialism. For Kaldor, crises like the one in Rwanda require the intervention of the benign forces of Western civilisation. Those forces were present at almost every stage in the tragedy of Rwanda, but it is hard to argue that they did anything to make the situation better. Unfortunately for Ken's argument in favour of the United Nations, it was precisely these forces which stood by while the slaughter happened.

The United Nations Assistance Mission for Rwanda (UNAMIR) was established after the ceasefire of 1993, with a mandate from the Security Council to 'contribute to the establishment and maintenance of a climate conducive to the secure installation and subsequent operation of a transitional government'.[44] The UN force made no attempt to stop the genocide. Its role was to try to secure the ceasefire between the rival armies. Again and again UN forces witnessed, but made no attempt to stop, the brutal murder of Tutsis and opposition figures. Even the general who headed UNAMIR was disgusted with their role.[45]

Even the limited role of UNAMIR was too much for America after the debacle of Somalia. On 21 April 1994 Madeleine Albright, then US ambassador to the UN, successfully proposed a Security Council resolution for UNAMIR to be scaled down by 90 percent, leaving 270 troops on the ground.[46] When a few weeks later the scale of the slaughter was becoming so great that calls were growing for renewed involvement, the US still resisted, delaying a vote and holding up the deployment of an African force by withholding the armoured cars needed. Members of the Clinton administration refused to describe the slaughter as genocide, as that would imply a legal obligation to do something about it.[47]

The forces of world capitalism had created the tragedy of Rwanda, but they could have no part in solving it. This fact is demonstrated by the role which French troops, despatched with UN approval, were to play in the coming months. Over the years France had invested considerable money and effort in cultivating a close relationship with the Hutu regime, and it was alarmed at what appeared to be the imminent takeover of RPF forces. In June, France was able to launch a military operation, dressed up as a humanitarian intervention, in an attempt to prop up its Hutu allies. The French troops of the bizarrely named Operation Turquoise were welcomed with open arms by the Hutu militias, by this time on the verge of defeat, who danced in the streets 'waving tricolour flags and carrying signs like "Welcome, French Hutus".'[48] The perpetrators of the genocide were protected in the French-occupied regions and treated as the legitimate representatives of the local government. The French intervention could only delay the victory of the RPF, but, in the words of Philip Gourevitch, 'the signal achievement of Operation Turquoise was to permit the slaughter of Tutsis to continue for an extra month, and to secure safe passage for the genocidal command to cross, with a lot of its weaponry, into Zaire'.[49]

With the victory of the RPF the genocide stopped, but another tragedy unfolded. The now ousted Hutu government had been able to portray the RPF as bent on genocide against the Hutus. There is little evidence that this is true, but the presence of Tutsi supremacists in its ranks cannot have given confidence to Hutu civilians. A mass exodus of Hutus to camps in Zaire and elsewhere began, but in amongst the refugees were activists, armed to the teeth and ready to relaunch a civil war. Under the protection of the UN High Commission for Refugees and the charitable NGOs which ran the camps in Zaire, the Hutu power activists were able to rearm and reorganise. They launched numerous raids across the border from Zaire, once again killing and maiming Tutsis.

Bosnia

Like Rwanda, Bosnia is one of the models for Kaldor's 'new wars' in which the west must intervene. But if we examine the crisis in Bosnia we find the US developing new strategies for maintaining its imperial dominance.[50] By 1995 the unanimity on the Security Council had effectively ended. It had become clear to the Russian ruling class that the US was not going to step in and solve their economic problems. Russia was again prepared to use its Security Council veto to thwart America's plans. It was at this point that America began to develop a new role for NATO.

In November 1995, the Dayton Peace Accord brought to an end the civil war in Bosnia, a war in which 200,000 to 300,000 Bosnians lost their lives. The peace deal was brokered almost exclusively by the US, who, in the words of Eric Hobsbawm, 'virtually single handed took over the task of peacemaking, and in the end virtually imprisoned the Balkan negotiators...for weeks in the depths of middle America, until they signed'.[51] The deal emerged after the balance of forces in the region swung decisively behind Croatia, which was a direct result of American led NATO intervention, repeatingly bombing Serbian positions and allowing the rapid advance of Croatian forces and the subsequent ethnic cleansing of Serbs from Krajina and sections of Bosnia.[52]

The peace plan cemented the ethnic partition of the region, with the land divided so that 49 percent of it went to a Serbian republic and 51 percent to a Bosnian-Croat federation. Initially the country would be run by a UN-appointed High Representative, who would oversee a gradual transition, over a three year period, to a genuine democracy. But the powers of the High Representative have been continually expanded as the Bosnian people have repeatedly elected representatives considered unsuitable by the international powers.[53] The UN High Representative, effectively a colonial governor, can write laws, veto political candidates in elections, and dismiss uncooperative elected members of Bosnian governing bodies. As time has gone on, far from moving towards democracy, the powers of UN appointees have become more and more dictatorial. Carlos Westendorp, the UN High Representative, described how the need to consult elected Bosnian representatives was removed in the following terms: 'You do not have power handed to you on a platter. You just seize it. If you use this power well, no one will contest it. I have already achieved this'.[54]

When asked why he thought none of the elected representatives supported the Federation as proposed by the UN, this is how Hans Schumacher, Senior Deputy High Representative, replied:

I don't care! I am simply not interested in who does not want the Federation: this is a concept which we will implement, despite the resistance in the field, which undoubtedly exists... We dictate what will be done! Therefore, this is a concept that will be implemented jointly and we simply do not pay attention to those who obstruct![55]

All the key positions are held by foreign appointees: the chief of the central bank is a New Zealander; the deputy chief of police comes from the discredited Los Angeles Police Department.

The US strategy in Bosnia has provided a model which it has since followed in Kosovo. It bypassed the Security Council in order to avoid the Russian and Chinese vetoes. A multinational NATO force, in reality dominated by US, was used to provide overwhelming firepower in order to impose the US's will on the ground. Once the US had imposed its preferred solution, the UN was used to provide legitimacy to the settlement.

The UN: the balance sheet

For most of its history the UN has been locked into passivity as a result of the standoff between the US and Russia. But what has emerged after the collapse of the old Stalinist command economies has not been some bright new organisation dedicated to the peace and humanitarian values of the charter. In Iraq the UN was used as a fig leaf for the greatest slaughter since the Second World War. In Somalia and Bosnia, where UN troops were sent in to 'keep the peace', its forces have in one case been responsible for mass slaughter, and in the other for the entrenchment of ethnic division in a partitioned state. In Rwanda UN-backed forces at first simply stood back whilst the slaughter took place, and then acted to protect the perpetrators of the genocide. In every case intervention has been portrayed as 'humanitarian', 'ethical' or 'benign', but in every case the policies of the Great Powers have been dictated by imperial design, not human rights or international law. The balance sheet destroys the arguments of liberal imperialists like Kaldor that intervention by the enlightened forces of the West can bring peace and human rights. Kaldor is merely rehashing Kipling's 'white man's burden' in a new guise.[56]

I am sure that Ken would agree with the bulk of my criticisms of the UN. His argument is not that the UN has been a success story, but that it can be reformed. However, there seem to be as many proposals for UN reform as there are commentators. It has been argued that Britain and France should give up their seats in favour of a single European Union representative. Others have argued that any one of a number of states deserve the status of permanent membership, including Japan, Germany, Indonesia, Brazil, Nigeria and India.[57] The Commission on Global Governance called for the expansion of the Security Council, the phasing out of the veto, and an increase in power for the General Assembly.[58]

Ken's suggestion that we can move towards Kant's vision of a peaceful world by vesting control of military forces in the Security Council is a variant of proposals put forward in different forms both by Boutros Boutros-Ghali in his 'Agenda for Peace' and by the Commission on Global Governance. Both called for peace enforcement units to be permanently available to be deployed by the Security Council.[59] It is not beyond the bounds of possibility that such a force could be established. But why should we have any illusions that an armed force controlled by the gangsters of the Security Council would behave any differently to armed forces controlled by its most powerful members? Armed forces exist, not to uphold human rights, but to suppress them in defence of the interests of state. Supranational armed forces are unlikely to behave any differently. The contradiction between the rhetorical commitments of the Declaration of Human Rights and the UN Charter's commitment to peace through the respect of sovereignty is a real one.

But practically, whatever reform of the UN is proposed, it comes up against the brick wall of the veto. The US and the other countries on the Council are not going to allow reform unless their predominance is protected. Even if we could reduce the role of the Great Powers, who would we replace them with? We cannot point to any country in the world that will do anything other than represent its national interests, or more accurately the interests of its ruling class:

> ...each member of the UN tries to use its membership to further its own interests. States have not joined out of respect for the 'UN idea', or with a view to creating a stronger organisation by transferring some of their powers to it. Rather they are in the UN for what they can get out of it. Of course, some states may see it as in their interests to increase the deference which is paid to the opinions of the UN—as expressed, particularly, in the resolutions of the General Assembly. This is likely to be much more true of the weaker than of the stronger members... But even weaker states show little sign of wanting to endow the UN with any general authority.[60]

As we approach the beginning of a new millennium, humanity can look back on the 20th century as one of almost unremitting wars and barbarism. In the 12 months to 1 August 1999 ten international wars and 25 civil wars were in progress, claiming 110,000 lives.[61] Given the scale of the slaughter it is not surprising that many cling to the hope that there is some institution which can stand above the conflicts and act to end them. For them, attacking the UN can seem to be the ultimate nihilism—if not the UN, then who will save us? Yet the 20th century also offers us the real alternative. In every decade of this century workers have made revolutions which have overturned their states and, even if only temporarily, held out the prospect of a world where humanity can live in peace without exploitation. It is only this tradition of working class self activity that can end the slaughter. This is not a call to passivity, a call to ignore the slaughter and wait for the glorious day of the revolution. It is vital that socialists today resolutely oppose every war led by our rulers, whether these wars are under the guise of their own nation states, NATO, the UN or any other institution.

Notes

My thanks go to Mike Haynes for his valuable comments on an earlier draft, and to Pete Waters and Carole Haines for their help in preparing this article.

1   R Cook, *The Guardian*, 5 May 1999; J Lloyd, *New Statesman*, 3 May 1999.
2   M Haynes, 'Theses on the Balkan War', *International Socialism* 83 (Summer 1999), p88.
3   M Kaldor, 'Disarmament: the Armament Process in Reverse', in E P Thompson (ed), *Protest and Survive* (Harmondsworth, 1980), p203.
4   *New Statesman and Society*, 30 January 1993. See also D Blackie, 'The United Nations and the Politics of Imperialism', *International Socialism* 63 (Summer 1994), p49, for a depressing list of ex-leftists who joined the warmongers of the Gulf War and Bosnia.
5   M Kaldor, 'If Peace Knows No Bounds, Why Should We?', *The Observer*, 18 July 1999.
6   Ibid.
7   Statement of the Helsinki Citizens' Assembly (Prague/The Hague, 6 March 1999), available at http://www.igc.apc.org/balkans/raccoon/hca-kos.html
8   *The Guardian*, 25 March 1999.
9   Although it is outside the scope of this article, I have to disagree with Ken's assertion that 'Yugoslavia had established a form of market socialism with self management, which functioned adequately', and his implication that this was the reason for US hostility to Milosevic's regime. The idea that the former Yugoslav state had anything to do with socialism should be anathema to socialists. It was the spectacular failure of market socialism which led to the current era of wars and instability. See M Haynes, 'The Nightmare of the Market', in L German (ed), *The Balkans, Nationalism and Imperialism* (London, 1999), p1, and D Blackie, 'Cauldron of Discontent', ibid, p20. It is not necessary to suggest any ideological motives for launching a war against the former Yugoslavia. The reasons were at once strategic (the desire to expand NATO influence through the Balkans) and economic (the need to protect the pipelines carrying oil from the huge deposits in the Caspian Sea). See J Rees, 'NATO and the New Imperialism', ibid, p173.
10   Charter of the United Nations, *Yearbook of the United Nations 1991* (Dordrecht, 1992), quoted in A Roberts and B Kingsbury (eds), *United Nations, Divided World* (Oxford, 1993), p499.
11   G Kolko, *The Politics of War* (New York, 1990), p242.
12   It is against this background that the infamous meeting between Churchill and Stalin of October 1944 can be understood. See G Kolko, op cit, p144.
13   P Kennedy, *The Rise and Fall of the Great Powers* (London, 1989), p459.
14   US Secretary of State Cordell Hull was a key advocate of free trade alongside an international security organisation which could resolve conflicts. What was implicit but remained unstated in his vision was the economic and military

dominance of the US, precisely the reason that Stalin and Churchill opposed him. See R Väyrynen, 'The UN and the Resolution of International Conflicts', in R A Falk, S S Kim and S H Mendlovitz (eds), *The United Nations and a Just World Order* (Boulder, 1991), p222.

15 G Kolko, op cit, p479.

16 D Horowitz, *The Free World Colossus* (London, 1965), p71. Horowitz has since repudiated this book. I am grateful to Mike Haynes for this point.

17 Commission on Global Governance, *Our Global Neighbourhood* (Oxford, 1995), p14.

18 'The UN's Role in International Society Since 1945', in A Roberts and B Kingsbury (eds), op cit, p6.

19 Ibid, p24.

20 R Väyrynen, op cit, p234.

21 M Bertrand, 'The Historical Development of Efforts to Reform the UN', in A Roberts and B Kingsbury (eds), op cit, p420.

22 See D J Whittaker, *United Nations in Action* (London, 1995), p28.

23 The contrast to Russia's invasion of Hungary that year could not be more complete. America used the same procedure to obtain an Assembly resolution condemning the invasion, which Russia simply ignored. See M Howard, op cit, p66.

24 See, for instance, B Boutros-Ghali, 'An Agenda for Peace', in A Roberts and B Kingsbury (eds), op cit, p470

25 J Rees, op cit, p173.

26 A Yoder, *The Evolution of the United Nations System* (London, 1993), p84.

27 For an insider's view of UN Security Council attitudes to the second Gulf War see A Parsons, *From Cold War to Hot Peace* (London, 1995), p55

28 The Soviets because they had no desire to see Iran's Islamic revolution cross the long border into the Soviet Empire. See A James, 'The United Nations', in D Armstrong and E Goldstein (eds), *The End of the Cold War* (London, 1990), p182.

29 A Parsons, op cit, p50.

30 L Humber, 'Left Wanting', *Socialist Review*, September 1990, p11; and D Blackie, op cit, p49.

31 A Parsons, op cit, p57.

32 The horror of the sanctions, and the contrast between the humanitarian mission statements of the UN and the reality on the ground, forced the UN Commissioner for Humanitarian Aid, Dennis Halliday, to resign, saying, 'I did not join the UN to wage war on children.' See S Smith, 'Oil on Troubled Waters', *Socialist Review*, February 1999, p11; and J Pilger, *New Statesman*, 3 May 1999, p35.

33 D Blackie, op cit, p57. A de Waal, 'US War Crimes in Somalia', *New Left Review* 230 (1998), p131.

34 A Parsons, op cit, p198.

35 A de Waal, op cit, p132.

36 D Blackie, op cit, p60.

37 At times the desperation and stupidity of the US forces became farcical, for example when US Rangers 'descended from helicopters through the roof of a building and seized eight members of the UN Development Programme'. A Parsons, op cit, p204.

38 A de Waal, op cit, p135.

39 Ibid, p131.

40 A de Waal, *Famine Crimes* (London, 1997), p179.

41 P Gourevitch, *We Wish to Inform You that Tomorrow we will be Killed with our Families* (London, 1999), p4.

42   C Kimber, 'Coming to Terms with Barbarism in Rwanda and Burundi',
      International Socialism 73 (Winter 1996), p127. N Davidson, 'The Trouble with
      Ethnicity', *International Socialism* 84 (Autumn 1999), p3.
43   C Kimber, op cit, p132.
44   A Parsons, op cit, p213.
45   P Gourevitch, op cit, p168.
46   Even that was too much for Albright, who wanted the forces reduced to zero. Ibid,
      p150.
47   Ibid, p152.
48   Ibid, p155.
49   Ibid, p160.
50   D Blackie, 'The Road to Hell', in L German (ed), op cit, p40; and M Haynes, 'The
      Nightmare of the Market', ibid, p1.
51   *The Independent*, 22 November 1995, quoted in G Jenkins, 'Peace by Partition',
      Socialist Review, December 1995, p9.
52   L German, 'The Balkan War: Can There be Peace?', in L German (ed), op cit, p99.
53   G Jenkins, 'Bosnia: The Great Carve Up', *Socialist Review*, May 1999, p15. The
      process is outlined in greater detail in D Chandler, *Bosnia Faking Democracy
      after Dayton* (London, 1999).
54   Ibid, p65.
55   Ibid, p75.
56   Kipling's poem was written in 1899, welcoming America's emergence as an
      imperial power with the conquest of the Philippines and Puerto Rico. The fact that
      humanitarian imperialism is the return of the 'white man's burden' in another
      guise is noted by Geoffrey Wheatcroft, who seems to welcome its return. See
      G Wheatcroft, *New Statesman*, 5 July 1999.
57   M Bertrand, op cit, p431. A Roberts and B Kingsbury, op cit, p39.
58   *Our Global Neighbourhood*, the report of the Commission on Global Governance,
      is one long argument for change to the UN system. The Commission was made up
      of the great and the good of parliamentarians, ex-government ministers and
      diplomats. Commission on Global Governance, op cit, pp225, 344.
59   B Boutros-Ghali, op cit, p470. Commission on Global Governance, op cit, p132.
60   A James, op cit, p187.
61   *The Guardian*, 22 October 1999.

Jesus: history's most famous missing person

JOHN ROSE

Just to set the right blasphemous tone, even if it's a little intellectually vulgar to do so, let's begin with Elvis rather than Jesus. A significant minority of Americans think it is possible that Elvis is still alive. And if you ever see those pictures from Gracelands, Elvis's former mansion, it's quite clear that many in the crowds that throng there have turned Gracelands into a sort of shrine. It is easy to mock those ageing rockers—'sad' is the word that comes to mind. Yet isn't what we are seeing mainly quite normal working class older men and women mourning the broken dreams of their youth?

Actually we have an example of this phenomenon much nearer to home, following the death of Princess Diana. *Socialist Worker* rightly dismissed the furore as mass hysteria but the paper also commented that the hysteria was rooted in what Marx once called alienation. Class society crushes most people's ability to discover in themselves genuine creative expression, so they find substitutes of all kinds, including turning the dead into icons of hero worship and symbols for their dreams and ideals for living. In any case, don't we have examples on the left? Che Guevara achieved a mythical status after his death, out of all proportion to his real contribution to world revolution. And, worse, much worse, there was once an extremely unpleasant orthodox Trotskyist group which became obsessed with something called Trotsky's death mask, many years after Trotsky's assassination. And all of this in the 20th century, in the age of humanism, science and rationality. Little wonder that 2,000 years ago it was a commonplace sort of thing.

When we try and enter that world of 2,000 years ago we need to remember that gods and god were taken for granted. Gods and god intervened daily in people's lives in all sorts of ways, or so people thought. A dream, a thunderstorm, an unexpected event, a sudden death, were immediately accorded religious and fatalistic significance. Also people became gods—especially Roman emperors.[1]

I use the phrase 'gods and god' deliberately. I want to avoid making the one-god belief necessarily more 'progressive' than the 'many-gods' belief. After all, think of world civilisation today. There is no question that the contribution of one-god Judaism and one-god Christianity and one-god Islam is enormous, but who can say that their contribution is greater than that from the multiple-god worlds of ancient Egypt, Greece and Rome, or for that matter the other religious cultures of Asia and Africa? However, the one-god idea is important. And I would like to refer in passing to the brilliant 20th century archaeologist and writer Gordon C Childe. Unusually for a man in his profession he was a Marxist, and his book *What Happened in History* rightly remains a classic. He made a fascinating observation about the Iron Age, the period approximately 2,500 years ago. He noted a common thread in the proliferation of new, more rational religions, including variations on one-god ideas, across the known world: Judaism, the Zoroastrianism of the Persians, and the rise of Buddha and Confucius in the Far East. At roughly the same time classical Athens had reached even beyond that to the beginnings of science.

Childe argues that the beginning of an idea of a common humanity was emerging and he linked it to the sudden relatively easy availability of cheap agricultural iron tools to till the land. Land productivity boomed. Goods traded as never before. Ideas exchanged and fused. New ideas, new ways of thinking and doing things, emerged. Societies began to develop from what Childe calls 'tribal barbarism'.[2] If Childe is right, then surely this is the turning point we should be celebrating at the end of the year—what happened 2,500 years ago, not the birth of a non-person 2,000 years ago. But more of that in a moment.

Actually the one-god idea is almost certainly even older. The British Museum houses, amongst the many wonderful artefacts it has stolen from other civilisations, some of the Armana letters. These are clay tablets, letters sent by the Egyptian pharaoh Akhnaten, some of which were sent to a Habiru people. There is a long debate as to whether these are Hebrew people. But the point here is that Akhnaten's sun-god worship anticipated one-god worship. (By the way, isn't sun worship eminently sensible?) Recent archaeological discoveries in Galilee in Israel from about 1,800 years ago have uncovered sun-god images on mosaic synagogue floors. Sun-god images on synagogue floors are almost unbelievable. After all, the Jewish religion specifically forbids idol worship. Sun worship falls into this category. There is a huge argument about the significance of these images—perhaps they are decoration. Nevertheless, what the debate tells us is something about being Jewish 2,000 years ago: that there were many different ways of being Jewish and worshipping one god.

For example, the Jews of Judaea, a small Roman province with the city of Jerusalem at its heart, worshipped their god in a way that was different to the Jews of Samaria, the province next door. The Jews of Samaria didn't even recognise the Jerusalem temple. They worshipped on a mountain. Again the Jews of Galilee had a tradition of fierce independence and rebelliousness. It was from Galilee, of course, that Jesus allegedly hailed. Additionally, there was a large Jewish diaspora throughout much of the Roman Empire—Jews mainly concentrated in urban centres, most famously in Alexandria and, of course, Rome itself. Finally, as the Jewish war against Rome developed, many quasi-Jewish religious-political parties developed, each with its own rules of being Jewish.

Two thousand years ago Rome was still struggling to assert its authority over Judaea. Its mechanism of rule through local ruling classes was proving to be exceptionally difficult because both the urban poor in Jerusalem and the peasantry in the outlying areas held Jerusalem's ruling class in utter contempt. Rome never really succeeded in subduing the region. Rebellion rumbled just beneath the surface for more than 50 years, occasionally breaking out into open revolt, and finally the full scale war of resistance both to Roman rule and its client Jewish ruling class, from between AD 66 and 70. It is not without significance that the first gospel, that of Mark, the first famous story of Jesus's life, was completed almost certainly in AD 70, the year the Romans crushed the resistance and destroyed the Jerusalem temple. Remarkably for this period, we have a detailed historical record by the Romanised Jewish historian Josephus. It is the only record of its kind. Any discussion of the period, including all serious academic discussion, is inevitably dominated by Josephus. Who was this extraordinary and obnoxious man?

First, he was a traitor. He was part of that corrupt Jerusalem ruling class that lacked authority amongst the Jewish poor. At first, and only because he had to, he supported the war of resistance. Indeed he was one of its leaders. But then he changed sides in a particularly obnoxious way. It seems he reneged on a suicide pact after an important military defeat: he literally walked into the arms of welcoming Roman generals! He was feted in Rome and even joined in the Roman celebrations after the final defeat of Jerusalem and the destruction of the temple. He writes approvingly of 'war trophies' displayed in Rome, including the sacred Menorah, the seven branch candleholder, stolen from the Jerusalem temple.[3]

Rome would sanction his new role as semi-official historian. His Greek language history of the Jewish revolt was written for the literati of the Roman Empire. Should we trust a word he writes? There are two points here. Firstly, his history tries to satisfy both a Roman audience and a Jewish one. Though this leads to fantastic distortions, the balancing act does impose a limited discipline. Secondly, there was a tradition of Greek and Roman history writing, which, whilst it had all kinds of propagandist and mystical flaws, nevertheless understood the significance of verifiable empirical evidence. Josephus certainly wanted to locate himself in this tradition.

But there is another reason why we need to take Josephus very seriously. A recent biographer, Tessa Rajak, has noted that Josephus's description of the Jewish revolt against Rome exposes a process familiar to modern historians. This is such an important point that it is worth quoting what she writes:

> As for the Jews of Palestine...there is every reason to believe they were becoming two nations...rich and poor... Once the two sides were in confrontation...[it conformed] in a startling way to the pattern and course of development of other revolutions, closer to us in time and incomparably better known to historians.[4]

She goes on to make a fascinating comparison with the different stages of the French Revolution, and the point is this: Josephus is spontaneously describing the dynamics of a real revolution. It is this that gives his account special authority.

But there is something else. How did his manuscript survive at all? It must have been copied dozens of times and kept and cherished by the earliest Christian monks who recognised it as a very important historical document, referring as it did to the times of Jesus. In fact they regarded the document as so important that they could not understand why there was no mention of the person of Jesus. Believing that Josephus had made a mistake, one of their number thoughtfully added in a brief reference! Not surprisingly this reference is the source of heated debate, but nearly all modern Christian historians and theologians now recognise it as a forgery. But let us praise the forger! He guaranteed the survival of the Josephus testimony to the Jewish revolution.

In truth Josephus did not notice this Jesus for a very good reason: because he almost certainly wasn't there. But Josephus did notice other Jewish rebels, some of them actually called Jesus—it was a very common name—and I will discuss some of them below. But first I want to look briefly at how modern scholarship is searching for the so called historical or 'real' Jesus. Geza Vermes is one of the Dead Sea Scroll scholars. He is part of a modern tradition that is reclaiming Jesus as a Jew. At the beginning of his book *Jesus the Jew* he argues that we should look for the man 'so distorted by Christian and Jewish myth alike...[who] was neither the Christ of the church, nor the apostate and bogeyman of Jewish popular tradition'.[5] Intriguingly modern Christianity is following the same path. The pope is stressing the Jewish roots of Jesus and the 'organic' bond linking Judaism to Christianity.[6] It's a bit late, given the nearly 2,000 year old Christian emphasis on the Jews killing Jesus. But this is not all. The Vatican is also distinguishing, and I quote from an official Vatican document, between the way 'Jesus presented himself to his contemporaries' and 'the way those who came to believe in Jesus...after the manifestation of him as one raised from the dead'.[7] But can this enlightened proposal to distinguish the life of Jesus from those who wrote about him after his death be sustained? Not really, for there is not a scrap of historically reliable evidence which is contemporary with his life. All the descriptions that matter come after his death, most famously in the gospels. An article, advising Christian educators on how to present the gospels in line with the kind of 'progressive' thinking just described, itself stresses the huge impact made on the gospel writers by the historical context in which they were writing.

The difficulty of liberating the 'real' Jesus from the context of the gospel writer draws the reader's attention because each gospel has a different 'real' Jesus. This requires a much more sophisticated analysis than is possible here, but here are a few examples. Mark's gospel 'seems very concerned with suffering and forcefully asserts that true insight into the person of Jesus is possible only by reckoning with his suffering and death'.[8] The author argues that it seems likely that this gospel was written during the immediate aftermath of the Jewish defeat and the destruction of the temple in AD 70. Thousands of Jewish rebels had just been crucified. Apocalyptic despair was the dominant mood. A good time to accept a messiah... The author makes the following point. In Mark's gospel, 'at the instant of Jesus's death, the curtain of the temple is torn asunder. This suggests...the eventual fate of the sacrificial cult'.[9] It is not difficult to see Christ on the cross as an alternative focus to the temple.

Matthew's gospel was probably written some 15 years later. Matthew's Jesus pays much greater respect to Jewish customs, food laws, sabbath as a day of rest, than did Mark's Jesus. So much is this the case that the author even argues that Matthew's Jesus 'embodies the entire history of Israel', likening Jesus delivering his Sermon on the

Mount to the scene of Moses on Mount Sinai. Why is this Jesus so Jewish? Because 'Matthew's community is a minority sub-group among various competing Jewish movements which are seeking to fill the vacuum created by the destruction of the temple'.[10]

Luke's gospel, probably written at a similar time to Mark's, has yet another Jesus. The author writes that Luke wants:

> *...to convince Rome that the church poses no threat...and ought to be granted legal status as a legitimate religion... [Hence] the family of Jesus is portrayed as law-abiding peasants from the Galilee... The adult Jesus responds to news about Pontius Pilate's latest atrocity, not by calling for revenge as Romans might expect from natives of troublesome Galilee, but by calling instead for repentance on the part of his fellow Jews... Pilate himself finds Jesus innocent of any crime... This positive portrayal of Romans has the welcome side effect of distancing the church from those Jews who had rebelled against Rome... Luke's Jesus is the healing saviour who brings reconciliation, forgiveness, wholeness and peace...*[11]

Before we leave the gospels, I want briefly to acknowledge Karl Kautsky's *The Foundations of Christianity*. Written at the beginning of the century, Kautsky's book became the standard Marxist authority on Christianity for several generations of socialists and communists. However, whether it stands up to contemporary standards of historical analysis of the ancient world, and in particular modern biblical criticism, is open to doubt, but in any case a judgement here is way beyond the scope of this article. Nevertheless, even the most superficial comparison of Kautsky's book with *The Class Struggle in the Ancient Greek World* by the Oxford Marxist scholar G E M de Ste Croix, published in the 1980s, illustrates the difficulty. De Ste Croix is obsessively scrupulous about sources, a research methodology requirement really quite absent in Kautsky's book. Anyway, Kautsky almost certainly exaggerated the 'communism' of the early Jewish Christians. But one thing he did quite brilliantly was to capture the way the gospels were forced at least partially to reflect the struggle between rich and poor.

Famously, only Luke's gospel mentions Lazarus, the poor man blessed by the Old Testament prophet Abraham, who in contrast damns the rich man. Again Luke's gospel has Jesus say in the Sermon on the Mount, 'Blessed be ye poor; for yours is the kingdom of god.' This is the same gospel where Jesus says it is easier for a camel to go through a needle's eye than for a rich man to enter the kingdom of god. In Matthew there is no Lazarus, and Jesus in the Sermon on the Mount blesses the poor only in *spirit*. 'All traces of class hatred are washed away with this adroit revisionism,' writes Kautsky,[12] as the early Jewish Christian groups began to adapt to the pacific norms of Roman society.

Finally, and again this brief comment cannot do it justice, mention must be made of the 'Gnostic gospels'. These gospels provide a very different version of the Jesus story. Unlike orthodox Judaism and Christianity, the 'chasm [which] separates humanity from the creator' is denied. 'Self knowledge is knowledge of god: the self and divine are identical'.[13] It may be that the early Christian leadership suppressed these gospels because of possible Hindu and Buddhist influence. As important, the doctrine of literal bodily resurrection is denied. According to one author, the doctrine may have come to 'serve a political function...legitimising the authority...of the [established] churches'.[14]

Let us turn now to what might be called the socio-economic, cultural, political and religious atmosphere of Judaea and Galilee in the 70 years from Jesus's alleged birth, roughly 2,000 years ago, to the fall of the Jerusalem temple. How did the gospel writers and others construct the Jesus personality out of this atmosphere? What is presented here is not at all systematic. All the sources are propagandist and anyway there are not many of them. Josephus dominates and then there are scraps from Roman, Jewish and Christian religious sources. So what we have is a sort of patchwork of characters and events in no particular order. Remember that we are in a pre-revolutionary and then a revolutionary situation. Religious ideas dominate and Jews expected the messiah.[15]

There were rebels and prophets, and Rome didn't particularly distinguish between the two. Both groups were regularly crucified as agitators. Josephus writes about false prophets and condemns them. But a prophet who is false for Josephus may be real enough for others. He describes that, at the moment the temple was about to fall to Rome, some 6,000 ordinary people (almost certainly he exaggerates the number) had been led there by a false prophet who had told them that god would make manifest the 'proofs of salvation'.[16] It was a suicide mission and they were all burnt to death.[17] But Josephus himself is ready to listen to prophets, false or otherwise. He goes on at length about all the signs that had been pointing to the fall of the temple: a star, a comet, a sacrificial cow giving birth, a chariot fight in the sky, and four years before the war a peasant called Jesus who prophesised day after day and night after night and loudly at festivals. He was regularly flogged for his prophesies but it didn't shut him up.[18] Josephus is also quite ready to see the Romans as god's agents punishing his people for polluting the temple.[19]

Again, earlier, as a younger man, Josephus reports that he had been ready to follow a hermit—he calls him Bannus—into the desert for three years.[20] Josephus's descriptions here have led to heated speculation amongst scholars about these stays in the desert. The Romans beheaded or crucified desert prophets. The famous Qumran Dead Sea Sect built a community in the desert to escape the moral pollution, and real corruption, of Jerusalem. Political rebels regrouped in the desert. Josephus describes an Egyptian (a 'most plausible candidate for would-be messiah'[21]) who led his followers out of the desert to march on Jerusalem and trusted divine aid sufficiently to face Roman heavy infantry. But to go from the sublime to the ridiculous, Josephus's biographer also notes that you could escape the Roman tax collector by going to the desert![22]

A constant source of agitation for both the Romans and the Jewish authorities in Jerusalem was Galilee. This is now the 'hot' subject for those in search of Jesus's historical roots. There is dispute about the Jews of Galilee 2,000 years ago. Were they recent converts? Had Jews emigrated there recently? There is agreement, though, that in Galilee being Jewish was different. The Jerusalem temple often seemed remote. Also we are talking about a mountain and peasant people with fertile lands and a fierce tradition of self sufficiency. There was real hostility to outside rulers, especially those who would tax them heavily.

As a doubtful leader of the Jewish revolt, Josephus was sent by Jerusalem to place himself at the head of the rebellion in Galilee. He seems enormously knowledgeable about its recent history. Josephus describes several generations of the same family all linked to the agitation. At the time of Jesus's alleged birth, there was Judas the Galilean who led the refusal to co-operate with the Roman census and hence avoid taxes. Forty years later two of his sons, Jacob and Simon, were crucified for revolutionary agitation. A surviving son, Menahem, later became one of the revolutionary leaders in Jerusalem. A nephew of Menahem, Eleazar, was the legendary captain at Masada, where a few hundred Zealots held out against the Romans after the fall of Jerusalem, which ended in mass suicide. (Incidentally, another name for Eleazar, like Jesus a very common name, may well be Lazarus.)

Was Judas a Zealot [23] or, as Josephus claims about him, a proponent of something called the 'fourth philosophy'? There is a scholarly argument about this which need not concern us here. That a revolutionary political-religious trend existed, there is no doubt. To quote from one of the most interesting books on the subject, the Oxford professor Martin Goodman's *The Ruling Class of Judaea: The Origins of the Jewish Revolt Against Rome AD 66-70*:

> *What Judas is said to have proposed was not just that subjection to Rome was evil but that acceptance of any human master was wrong since Jews should be ruled by god alone... The effect of this ideology was anarchy and political revolution.*[24]

> *Some Jews seem to have believed that* [such] *violence was divinely ordained.*

The most compelling motive for any Jew to join in violent struggle was a belief that the messianic age was not just a future hope...but a present actuality. Once the messiah had arrived and the last battles, so graphically imagined in the Qumran War Scroll, were ready to commence...[you] had no choice but to participate.[25]

Josephus cites the belief in the messiah 'as a main cause of revolt'.[26]

De Ste Croix has emphasised the hatreds between city and countryside 2,000 years ago. He notes that the Jesus of the gospels is first and foremost a peasant preacher in country villages in Galilee.[27] The city would take as much food as it could from the countryside. In turn the peasants would secretly store as much as they could. For the peasants of Galilee purity, religious and moral, lay in the countryside. Vermes has also analysed the Jewish religious literature of the time and has provided examples of peasants from Galilee trying to sell their goods in the Jerusalem marketplace and merchants making fun of their Galilean accents![28] Even the very word for peasant carries an added insulting twist. Vermes quotes Talmudic sources where the word for peasant implies an unclean animal.[29] And again he quotes the gospel of John where someone expresses amazement that the messiah could come from Galilee.[30]

The search for the Galilean roots of Jesus may not have found him, but has at least uncovered a tradition of unorthodox Jewish charismatic healers. Hanina ben Dosa is one of them. His name first appears in the Mishnah (a collection of legal teachings).[31] The religious texts report that his power in prayer was so great that he could withstand a deadly snake bite. He was renowned as a healer. Though distrusted at the Jerusalem temple, he was sent for when the son of a leading Jerusalem religious leader was struck by a mortal fever. Hanina ben Dosa prayed and the boy was cured.[32] His healing gifts were linked to his piety and hatred of money. Sin and sickness were thought to be linked.[33] In this tradition, poverty is almost holy and a healer who chooses it enhances his gifts. This is a tradition linked with the Old Testament prophet Isaiah.[34] A contemporary of ben Dosa is reported as saying that men like him are 'men of truth hating evil gain'—'they hate their own money and all the more the money of other people'.[35]

We turn now to the revolt in Jerusalem itself. First the background. The temple building was magnificent and drew pilgrims from all over the Jewish diaspora—which was already well developed throughout the towns and cities of the Roman Empire. Jerusalem was a very affluent city—building work, handicrafts and trade provided employment for empoverished peasants from the countryside. Unique to the Jewish religion was a tradition of charity which Christianity borrowed wholesale. Though, unlike the ben Dosa version of Judaism, it is the rich giver of money to the poor who was made to feel sacred, even though he still remained very rich.[36] However, the charity was important. It kept far more people alive than would otherwise have been the case. There was then a large urban poor population mixing with a large pilgrim population. Its discontent remained a perpetual threat to rulers, Jewish and Roman. The Jewish ruling class notoriously could not keep order. Furthermore, the rich were getting richer and the poor poorer. Recent archaeological digs have revealed just how enormous were the houses of the Jerusalem rich 2,000 years ago.[37] Josephus explicitly identifies class hatred as a cause of the revolt.[38] Indeed he is shocked by the eagerness of the poor to kill the rich and take their property. There are then two struggles: Jews against Roman rulers and poor Jews against rich Jews.

The Greek word 'stasis' figures prominently: it means 'internal strife'. In part this reflects the faction fighting amongst the leaders of the revolt; but it also reflects the poor Jews' persistent mistrust of the richer leaders of the revolt. The Roman historian Tacitus was astonished at how bitter was the stasis even as the Roman army closed in on Jerusalem in AD 70.[39] In the pre-revolutionary period sometimes the strife was used to pressurise the Jewish leadership to stand up to Rome. Thus Josephus tells us that when Pontius Pilate—yes, it is he, the most senior Roman official involved in the Jesus crucifixion myth—ordered shields bearing the emperor's image into Jerusalem, mass action forced their removal.[40] Again, when the particularly obnoxious emperor Caligula ordered his statue to be placed in the Jerusalem temple, Josephus reports that a strike, a full scale withdrawal of labour, stopped it.[41]

One of the first acts of the revolt was the burning of the debt archives in the temple. A peasant would borrow money from a rich Jerusalem based landowner. Then he would find he couldn't afford the interest on the debt.[42] Thus the landlord would eventually acquire the peasant's plot of land, turning the peasant into a landless labourer—and quite possibly into a bandit, joining bandit gangs of ex-peasants who couldn't afford to pay taxes.[43] The challenge to money-power at the heart of temple life is surely symbolised in the Jesus myth, when he challenges the money changers in the temple. A landless labourer could also end up as a debt-bond slave. Matthew's gospel has a parable about a debt-bond slave sold with his wife and children.[44]

The most famous bandit leader is Barabbas—in jail with Jesus. The Jewish scholar Hyam Maccoby wrote a very exciting book about Jesus and the Jewish revolt, in the aftermath of 1968, where he identifies Jesus as Barabbas.[45] Unfortunately, this book is not taken seriously. Josephus describes several other bandit chiefs, Robin Hood figures, including a Jesus of Galilee.[46] Some of them are given confirmation in the Rabbinical literature. Archaeological evidence supports the possibility of bandit caves linked to particular impoverished villages[47]—providing a sort of 'United Nations' style humanitarian food aid service with supplies robbed from the rich! The Zealots recruited some these bandits to help strengthen their power base in Jerusalem;[48] some of them may have been the *sicarri*, the dagger men, who would merge with crowds, with daggers concealed, and then assassinate enemies of the revolution.

What are we to make of the Zealots? The word has carried into modern times as a term of abuse meaning 'fanatic'. The French Revolutionary Jacobins and of course the Bolsheviks suffered this abuse, but we should ignore it. It is tempting to see the Zealots as the best organised revolutionary party in the city. It seems they were the best organised defenders of the city and they minted some of the best coins of the revolt[49] with their 'Freedom' slogan which remains subject to intense speculation as to its religious or secular meaning.[50] Intriguingly, when they seized the temple they selected a new high priest by lottery, deliberately avoiding candidates from the traditional ruling class families. The high priest chosen was a village stonemason, probably the first ever high priest from such lowly origins—dismissed by Josephus as a boor and ignoramus![51]

Tessa Rajak, in her biography of Josephus, adds that his assessment here has been too easily accepted by scholars, despite a more favourable Talmudic interpretation.[52] The trouble is that our dependence on Josephus makes any definitive judgement about the Zealots really difficult. There is a sensational example of why this is so. Josephus provides a brilliant description of the last stand against the Romans at Masada which ends in mass suicide. He puts a long speech advocating suicide into the mouth of the Zealot leader Eleazar. The speech is a hugely powerful defence of freedom. Yet there is a very plausible view that Josephus invented or at least magnified the whole thing, to make up for his own appalling behaviour in the Jewish revolt![53]

I want to conclude by drawing one possible hypothesis from the events described: that the Jesus myth only takes root, and is connected to, the fall of the temple. In describing the New Testament Chris Harman, in his *A People's History of the World*, puts it like this:

> On the one hand, there was the sense of revolutionary urgency, of immanent (in the religious sense) transformation, that came from the Jewish rebels in Palestine before the destruction of Jerusalem, the vision of the apocalypse and the reign of the 'saints'. The high and mighty being pulled down and the poor and humble ruling in their place... Yet at the same time by projecting the transformation into the future and into a different eternal realm to that of earth, the revolutionary message was diluted.[54]

It was diluted to appeal across social class boundaries in the Jewish diaspora throughout the Roman Empire. How this may have occurred is the subject of a key chapter in Chris Harman's book.

A key figure, perhaps *the* key figure, almost certainly a real historical character, who promotes the Jesus myth and helps build the early Christian communities in the Jewish diaspora, is Paul, formerly Saul, who saw the blinding light[55] and converted on the road to Damascus. Paul began preaching long before the fall of the temple, assuming the dating of his letters is accurate. He is fixated on the crucifixion and the resurrection, though he never describes Jesus's life.[56] It's possible, of course, that he anticipates the fall of the temple—according to Josephus others had made such a prophecy. Anyway, this Greek speaking diaspora Jewish artisan, possibly a tentmaker, was impressed by the relatively large numbers of Gentiles, disaffected urban middling groups, traders, artisans and beggars who were attracted to the Jewish religion throughout the Roman Empire. They were the 'god fearers', non-Jews who were not prepared to undergo circumcision and abide by the food laws and other Old Testament injunctions. By helping to abolish what appeared to be exclusive restrictions in Judaism, Paul made conversion easier, but in the process helped to invent a different religion. Also, some of the cults of local religions—so called pagan religions—were incorporated. According to Chris Harman the early (Jewish) Christians were driven 'by greater than usual sensitivity to the insecurities and oppression of life in the empire's cities... The New Testament credits the apostle with "speaking in tongues"—with ecstatic speeches which give expression to their innermost feelings. It was in such a state that they were likely to synthesise a new religious vision out of elements from older ones'.[57] But this was also an appeal to all social classes. As Paul put it, a slave could stay with his master even if they were brothers in Christ. And, arguably, this set the seal on the way Christianity would evolve.

Notes

1   'The notion that a ruler might be a god was by no means curious to Romans. After the death of Julius Caesar the Senate recognised him as a god, and a temple was dedicated to him in 29 BC. Octavian, his adopted son, exploited the relationship with enthusiasm, proclaiming himself on his coins as Divifilius, the son of god.' M Goodman, *The Roman World (44BC-AD180)* (Routledge, 1997).

2   Gordon C Childe, *What Happened in History* (Penguin, 1985), p221.

3   T Rajak, *Josephus* (Duckworth, 1983), pp168-173, 218-219.

4   Ibid, p26.

5   G Vermes, *Jesus the Jew* (SCM Press, 1983), p17.

6   P Cunningham, 'The Synoptic Gospels and their Presentation of Judaism', in D Efroyinson, E Fisher and L Klenicki (eds), *Within Context: Essays on Jews and Judaism in the New Testament* (Collegeville, 1993), p42.

7   Pontifical Biblical Commission instruction (1984), quoted ibid, p43.

8   Ibid, p47.
9   Ibid, p50.
10   Ibid, p55.
11   Ibid, pp57-58.
12   K Kautsky, *The Foundations of Christianity* (Russell & Russell, 1953), p279.
13   E Pagels, *The Gnostic Gospels* (Pelican, 1985), p19. I am grateful to Michael Rosen for drawing my attention to the Gnostic gospels.
14   Ibid, p38.
15   M Goodman, *The Ruling Class of Judaea* (Cambridge University Press, 1995), p1.
16   T Rajak, op cit, p90.
17   M Goodman, *The Ruling Class of Judaea*, op cit, pp90-91.
18   T Rajak, op cit, p91.
19   Ibid, pp94-95.
20   Ibid, pp37-38.
21   M Goodman, *The Ruling Class of Judaea*, op cit, p93.
22   T Rajak, op cit, p38.
23   G Vermes, op cit, p47.
24   M Goodman, *The Ruling Class of Judaea*, op cit, pp93-94.
25   Ibid, pp91-92.
26   Ibid, p89; and T Rajak, op cit, p141.
27   G E M de Ste Croix, *The Class Struggle in the Ancient Greek World* (Duckworth, 1983), p427; and G Vermes, op cit, p48.
28   G Vermes, op cit, p52.
29   Ibid, pp54-55.
30   Ibid, p5.
31   Ibid, p73.
32   Ibid, p75.
33   Ibid, pp58-72.
34   M Goodman, *The Ruling Class of Judaea*, op cit, p130.
35   G Vermes, op cit, p7.
36   M Goodman, *The Ruling Class of Judaea*, op cit, p64-65.
37   Ibid, p5.
38   Ibid, p13.
39   Ibid, p20.
40   Ibid, pp45-46.
41   Ibid, p7.
42   Ibid, pp57-154.
43   Ibid, pp60-61.
44   T Rajak, op cit, p119, fn 40.
45   H Maccoby, *Revolution in Judaea: Jesus and the Jewish Resistance* (Ocean Books, 1973).
46   M Goodman, *The Ruling Class of Judaea*, op cit, p63.
47   Ibid, pp63-64.
48   Ibid, p225.
49   Ibid, p201, fn3.
50   T Rajak, op cit, p139; and M Goodman, *The Ruling Class of Judaea*, op cit, pp17-19.
51   T Rajak, op cit, p133.
52   Ibid, p13. Martin Goodman also dismisses the High Priest as a nonentity, p186.
53   M Goodman, *The Ruling Class of Judaea*, op cit, p214; T Rajak, op cit, p220.
54   C Harman, *A People's History of the World* (Bookmarks, 1999), p93.
55   M Goodman, *The Roman World (44BC-AD180)*, op cit, pp319-320.
56   Ibid, p20.
57   C Harman, op cit, p95.

The 20th century: an age of extremes or an age of possibilities?

CHRIS HARMAN

'The most terrible century in Western history.' 'A century of wars and massacres.' 'The most violent century in human history'.[1]

The quotes are from one of Britain's best known liberal philosophers, a radical French agronomist and a conservative Nobel prize winner for literature. They are brought together at the beginning of Eric Hobsbawm's history of the world since 1914, which is titled, appropriately, *The Age of Extremes*. They sum up a century which has seen bloodletting and barbarity on an immense scale—20 million dead in the First World War, 40 million dead in the Second World War, 6 million exterminated in the Nazi death camps, 10 million imprisoned, many to die, in Stalin's *gulags*, 4 million dead in the famine he brought to the Ukraine and Kazakhstan, another 4 million dead in the famine which British rule brought to Bengal in the early 1940s, hundreds of thousands burnt alive in the bombing of Dresden, Hamburg, Hiroshima and Nagasaki, a million killed in the French colonial war in Algeria, 2 million in the US war in Vietnam and Cambodia, millions more killed and forced to flee as refugees in the wave of civil wars that swept Africa, the Caucasus, Central America and the Balkans in the 1980s and 1990s. The century began with the barbarity of the Boer War (in which Africans and Boers alike died in their thousands in British concentration camps) and the Belgian enslavement of the Congo; it ended with the barbarity of ethnic cleansing and aerial bombing in the Balkans and south east Turkey.

Historians can debate endlessly whether the century was absolutely more horrible than the 14th century in Europe, when the first great crisis of feudalism led to a halving of the population through famine, plague, war and civil war, or than the 17th century, when the devastation of the Thirty Years War reduced the population of central Europe by about a third. But the absolute level of privation, misery, violence and killing is not the real issue. What is horrifying about the 20th century is that this was the first century in human history—or at least since the move from hunter-gathering to agriculture some 10 millennia ago—in which the material means existed to give everyone a better, hunger and disease-free, more fulfilling life. It was the century of previously unimaginable technological change that opened up the prospect of ending forever the backbreaking toil that had been the fate of the mass of humanity. Yet the century saw the technology used to terrorise, dehumanise and kill on an unprecedented scale.

People in the 1890s had not thought it would be like this. A cult of progress dominated much of intellectual life and popular opinion. It certainly exercised a growing sway over the socialist movements of the time. This can be seen by looking at the debate which took place within the German movement over reform and revolution, between Eduard Bernstein, Karl Kautsky and the young Rosa Luxemburg. Bernstein felt able to claim that existing capitalist society was inevitably becoming more peaceful, more crisis-free, more humane, more egalitarian and more democratic.

In all advanced countries we see the privileges of the capitalist bourgeoisie yielding step by step to democratic organisations... The common interest gains in power to an increasing extent as opposed to private interest and the elementary sway of economic forces ceases.[2]

This process could come to fruition without the 'dissolution of the modern state system'.[3] All that was necessary was a further spread of parliamentarianism, with socialists embracing a thoroughgoing 'liberalism'[4] and a policy of piecemeal reform within the existing system.

Karl Kautsky, the party's main theorist, denounced Bernstein's argument. Capitalism, he insisted, could not be reformed out of existence; at some point there had to be a 'struggle for power' and a 'social revolution'. But his practical conclusions were not very different to Bernstein's. The socialist revolution would come about, he argued, through the inevitable growth of the party vote, as the working class and the scientific intelligentsia alike saw the need for change.

Both Bernstein and Kautsky shared the optimistic 'scientism' or 'positivism' of the middle class intelligentsia and believed in the mechanical inevitability of progress. For Bernstein, science, technology and increasing democracy were turning capitalism into socialism in the here and now. Kautsky saw the process as taking place in the future, not the present, but he was just as certain about its mechanical inevitability: throughout history, changes in the forces of production had always, eventually, led to changes in the relations of production, and they would do so now, if people only waited patiently. Neither Bernstein nor Kautsky suspected that barbarism was being prepared alongside the prerequisites for socialism.

Rosa Luxemburg's contribution to the debate was the most far-seeing. She insisted that the very processes which Bernstein saw as democratising, civilising and moderating capitalism were leading to a new period of great crisis and imperialist conflicts. There is no doubt that the 20th century vindicated Luxemburg and proved how facile Bernstein's position was—and the position of those who, in one way or another, have resurrected the notion of inevitable conflict-free progress since, from Anthony Crosland, John Strachey and Daniel Bell in the 1950s[5] to Francis Fukuyama in the early 1990s. But even Luxemburg could not foresee in the 1890s the full horror of the century ahead. There is still a tone of the inevitability of socialism in her writings;[6] it was not until she was faced with the mad delirium of the First World War that she returned to a formula of Frederick Engels—'socialism or barbarism'. And by barbarism she did not just mean barbarity, but something more and worse—the destruction of civilisation and culture, as had taken place at the time of the collapse of the Roman Empire in the west.[7]

Recognising the recurrent barbarity of the 20th century is one thing, explaining it another. Not, of course, that everyone is prepared even to recognise it. It hardly fits into the Third Way. I don't believe there is a Barbarity Zone in the Millennium Dome alongside the Spirit Zone and the Money Zone. Nevertheless, the mainstream thinkers quoted earlier have recognised this barbarity, and so does a lot of mainstream history. It is to be found, for instance, in several episodes of the BBC TV series *A People's Century*. The problems arise when it comes to integrating the horror into the rest of the picture. It all too easily can appear as a purely irrational aberration, as some inexplicable product of the human psyche, or as a product simply of deranged individuals—of Mussolini and Hitler in the inter-war years, or of Saddam Hussein and Slobodan Milosevic in the 1990s: the 'great man' theory of history gives way to the 'evil man' theory of history. It can even be seen as the result of the attempt to recast society so as to get rid of its horrors—this was the explanation of people like Talmon (in *The Rise of Totalitarian Democracy*) and Popper (in *The Poverty of Historicism* and *The Open Society and its Enemies*) 40 or 50 years ago. More recently it has been the explanation of influential postmodernists, for whom totalitarianism is the product of totalising theories. Rousseau and Marx get the blame for Hitler and Stalin—and, presumably, Saddam Hussein and

Slobodan Milosevic (such theorists forget, of course, the horror perpetrated by Henry Kissinger and encouraged by Madeleine Albright).

The one approach to history that should be able to explain the 20th century is Marxism. There have been several very important works on aspects of the century inspired by Marxism—above all Trotsky on 1905 and 1917, but also lesser writers like Harold Isaacs on the Chinese revolutions of the 1920s, Angelo Tasca (writing under the name Rossi) on the rise of Italian fascism, C L R James on the revolution in Haiti, Broué on the German Revolution of 1918-1923 and the Spanish Revolution of 1936, Deutscher's biographies of Trotsky and Stalin. But there has been an absence of attempts to provide an overview of worldwide developments. This is partly because, as we should never forget, the first generation of 20th century Marxists usually ended up murdered—Rosa Luxemburg, Trotsky, Bukharin, Andres Nin, Radek, Hilferding, Volosinov and scores of others, or driven to premature deaths like Gramsci. It was also to a large extent a product of Stalinism: looking at the present might lead to unpleasant challenges to the party line, and so the best British Marxists looked at the 17th, 18th and early 19th centuries, the best French ones at the heroic years 1789-1794.

The one recent exception is Eric Hobsbawm's *The Age of Extremes*. It is probably the most accessible account of the century, providing a total vision which combines economics, politics, science and art. It is, for instance, much more successful by being more coherent than the BBC's *A People's Century*. It is seductive in its ambition and riveting in its drive. Yet it is also defective in a central way that is easy not to notice. I remember when I read it, to do a review for *Socialist Worker*, I noticed on all sorts of points of detail it was mistaken. I also thought it was fundamentally wrong on Stalinism. But I thought it provided an overview of the century which would be of immense value to people. What I did not really grasp until I began work on my own book, *A People's History of the World*, was what was missing from it.

On the face of it, Hobsbawm's book seems to be in the classic Marxist tradition—of relating 'base' and 'superstructure', of 'history from below' and 'history from above'. It connects global economic trends of slump and boom, the rise and fall of political movements (its 'extremes'), intellectual fashions, changes in popular culture. In doing so it seems very different to much recent academic Marxist history, which has dealt simply with particular movements through 'history from below', without connecting them with wider, global trends. This means he conveys something missing from much academic Marxism, a sense of the system's repeated lurches towards barbarism—1914, 1929, 1933, 1939 and, it is implied at the end, the early 21st century.

What is missing, however, is any real notion of an alternative to this, apart from trying to hold fast to what exists at present. Faced with the First World War, Hobsbawm's conclusion is to bemoan the split in the working class movement between openly reformist and revolutionary wings. Faced with the rise of Nazism and fascism in the 1930s, the only hope for him was with the Popular Front movements concocted in France and Spain, even through they failed miserably in their goal (the Popular Front majority elected to the French National Assembly in 1936 voted Pétain to power in 1940). Faced with the domination of Europe by German Nazism, the only alternative lay in an alliance of socialists with British and US capitalism and Russian Stalinism—although the alliance led to Hiroshima, Nagasaki, the Cold War, the Korean War, the Algerian War and the Vietnam War. He justifies this by claiming that the choice was 'between what in the 19th century would have been called 'progress and reaction'.[8] Faced with the horror of the 20th century, the alternative, it seems, was to...move back to the methods of the 19th century! The choice of socialism or barbarism becomes 'bourgeois democracy or barbarism'. The centre cannot hold—and so we must all rush to the centre!

Socialism does get a mention through much of the book. But it is the socialism of the Russia (and to a lesser extent China, Vietnam and Cuba) which is seen as still embodied in Stalinism and dying with the events of 1989-1991: four revolutions and a long drawn out funeral. And, even here, the force classical Marxism saw as the historical protagonist of socialism hardly appears. The Russian Revolution receives a very positive treatment (a welcome contrast to so much ignorant historical gibberish which has paraded as a history of the revolution since 1989); but the factory workers and the soviets (workers' councils) which were key to it get only a couple of passing mentions.

This is no isolated aberration. The working class is the great missing link throughout Hobsbawm's book. It hardly appears at all in the first half of the book, and finally makes its appearance towards the end to be discussed solely in terms of lifestyle. An index is often a good guide to a book's subject matter. There are only four references in the *The Age of Extremes'* index to trade unions. There are no references to such key expressions of working class power in the 20th century as the Spanish CNT, the American CIO, the French CGT, the Central Budapest Workers Council; the Polish Solidarnosc is mentioned once. From this history you would never imagine that the occupation of factories was a key turning point in post First World War Italian history or the sit-ins of June 1936 in 1930s French history. Even the huge concentrations of workers which characterised much of 20th century capitalism are missing: the River Rouge plant, Renault Billancourt, FIAT Mirafiori, the Lenin shipyard in Gdansk.

In the previous volume of Hobsbawm's history, *The Age of*

Imperialism, the working class did get a chapter. But in *The Age of Extremes* it is absent. It is as if Hobsbawm's attitude to the working class is same as that which Marx says the bourgeoisie has towards history: it has been, but is no more. In fact, even in the previous volume, the working class was a secondary factor. Hobsbawm wrote of the period leading up to the First World War:

> *So far as the core countries of bourgeois society were concerned, what destroyed the stability of the belle époque was the situation in Russia, the Hapsburg Empire and the Balkans, and not in western Europe or even Germany. What made the British political situation dangerous on the eve of the war was not the rebellion of the workers, but the division within the ranks of the rulers.*[9]

Hobsbawm's whole approach is to look at big politics and big economics simply in terms of bitter rows within ruling classes and between states. But the politics of such rows are incomprehensible without looking all the time at how successful rural rulers are in wresting resources from the rest of society—that is, at their struggles to extract a surplus from the exploited classes. The drive of British, French and German capitalisms towards war in 1914 is incomprehensible without looking at this. It is what underlay their rows over spheres of influence, empires, support for client states, and so on. Similarly, you cannot begin to understand why the German ruling class embraced Hitler *after* his vote had fallen by 2 million in the elections of the autumn of 1932, or why it allowed him to embark on the policies which led to the Second World War, unless you start with its concern with the surplus.

But the other side of this is recognising as a central, not marginal, fact of the 20th century the way in which upsurges of working class revolt throw their politics into disarray. You can describe certain aspects of 20th century economics, politics, art and culture without seeing this. But you cannot grasp their inner connection. For that you have to see how key moments of class struggle influence the parameters within which everything else occurs. Such key moments were the syndicalist wave before 1914; the succumbing of workers to war in 1914; the revolutions in Russia 1917 and Germany 1918-1919; the occupation of factories in 1920 and the defeat of Italian workers in the two years after; the defeat of the union drive in steel in the US in 1919 and the collapse of the triple alliance in Britain in 1920; the rise and defeat the anti-colonial movements in Egypt, India, China, Ireland and Morocco in 1919-1927; the collapse of the German workers' movement in the face of Nazism in 1933; the upsurge of the workers' movements in France in 1934-1936; the rise of the CIO in 1936; the rising against the Francoist coup in Spain in July 1936; the containment of movements from below after 1936 opening the way to the Second World War; the resistance movements in Greece, Poland, Italy and, to a lesser extent, France; the containment of movements after the war; the victories of the anti-colonial movement in India and of the People's Liberation Army in China; the solidification of the Cold War structure with the defeats and splitting of the workers' movements in France, Italy and Greece; the anti-Stalinist risings of 1953 and 1956; the workers' and students' movement of 1968; the anti-Francoist strikes of 1974-1976, and the Portuguese Revolution of 1974-1975.

To provide an account of the 20th century which misses out these moments is to have the play *Hamlet* not only without the Prince of Denmark, but also without Ophelia, Claudius, Horatio, Gertrude, Polonius, and even Rosencrantz and Guildenstern. Yet most of them are missing from Hobsbawm's book, as much as from any conventional history of the century. There is not even the sense that, at minimum, class struggle always, at every point, lays down limits within which the system operates. Still less is there any awareness that there were points when workers were close to breaking through. For Hobsbawm, the class-in-itself rarely makes its presence felt; the class-for-itself, never.

The 20th century was the century in which capitalism truly became a global system. There had been a global market before that. But most of the participants in that market were pre-capitalist ruling classes or small producers controlling their own means of production; it is worth remembering that until the 1940s a huge proportion of the world's population were still subsistence farmers, capable of surviving on their own produce even if they had to sell some of their crops to pay rents and taxes. It is only with the 20th century that you see the relentless spread of production based on wage labour to embrace the whole globe. In 1900, of the world's population of some 1000 million, perhaps 50 million were wage workers; of today's population of 6,000 million, probably more than 2 billion are.

The more wage labour spreads, the more the only source of surplus becomes its exploitation, rather than the extraction of rents and taxes from the peasantry; today there are very few countries in which the majority of national income is still produced in agriculture, and a growing portion of agriculture is capitalist agriculture, even in Third World countries. Under these circumstances, success—and sometimes even survival—for any ruling class depends on reducing labour costs by keeping a lid on wages and forcing up productivity. The labour costs which matter are not just those of 'traditional' manual workers, but also of people in occupations that were still regarded at the beginning of the century or even in the 1950s as 'middle class'—clerical workers of all sorts, technicians, teachers and lecturers, nurses. Forms of work supervision and payment systems that were confined to groups of manual workers a century ago are now being introduced across the board under the guises of 'flexibility', 'payment by results', 'market testing' and so on. There is a homogenisation of conditions and in consequence, to some extent, of lifestyles. Marx in 1843 first referred to workers as 'the universal class'. In fact, it is only at the end of the 20th century that such a class begins to exist worldwide as more than a relatively small proportion of the population.

Under such circumstances, the whole system is marked, as never before, by the flows of alienated wage labour. Unless you map these flows, you cannot see the logic of the system—and the logic of conflict between classes within the system. Mainstream historians and sociologists do not do this. Historians do not see that these flows underlie the contingencies of economic, political and social history; sociologists mistake form for content, and see the proletarianisation of the working conditions of the salaried middle classes as an embourgeoisiment of the lifestyles of the working class. Hobsbawm falls into both traps. His is a history which has room for some of the mechanical contrivances used by the system and for the lifestyles of some of the people within it, but no room for the connecting links—the pumping out of surplus value, the distribution of surplus value within the ruling class, the accumulation of surplus value, the waste of surplus value. It therefore has no room for explaining either the centrality of class conflict or the dynamic of class conflict.

This is not just a matter of the past, but also of the future. The barbarities of the 20th century were not just confined the period 1914-1945. Even the 'golden years' for the advanced industrial countries during the long boom of the 1950s and 1960s were accompanied by horrific wars against parts of the Third World and by the piling up of the means of mass destruction. We were promised, with the collapse of the Eastern bloc and the end of the Cold War at the end of the 1980s, 'an end of history', with a 'New World Order' and a 'peace dividend'. Instead the 1990s witnessed economic collapse in much of the former Eastern bloc, a prolonged recession in Europe and Japan, a rash of civil wars, the aerial bombing of Baghdad and Belgrade, and a profound economic crisis across East Asia; at the time of writing there is endless speculation among mainstream economists as to how long the US stock exchange boom can keep going, and what the implications for the world as a whole are if it collapses. The emergence in major western European countries as a serious force of fascist parties that used to be regarded as a near joke suggests that the ghosts of the 1930s are far from vanquished.

On top of all this, there are new threats never imagined in the first half of the century. An epidemic disease, AIDS, is slashing into life expectancy in wide areas of Africa and threatening to engulf much of Asia too; yet those who control the world's wealth refuse to release the relatively low level of funds needed to bring it under control, and the great pharmaceutical companies do not see it as worthwhile to invest any great sums in looking for a vaccine against it (or, for that matter, against that old enemy, malaria). The endless pumping of carbon dioxide and other 'greenhouse' gases into the atmosphere is beginning to radically destabilise the world's climate, threatening both to flood major inhabited areas and to upset the balance of world food supplies; every major government acknowledges the threat; every major government continues with transport, energy and industrial policies which increase the level of greenhouse gases and the danger of a worldwide disaster. Finally, advances in technology continue to be transmuted into increased levels of destructive weaponry; the greatest economic military power, the US, has resumed the search for a 'Star Wars' anti-missile system which will free it from the fear of retaliation if it ever launches a nuclear 'first strike'; a whole range of lesser, medium size powers are trying to develop their own 'micro' means of mass destruction to threaten each other with and to deter the US (or its nuclear client state, Israel) from one day threatening them with the aerial bombardment used against Baghdad and Belgrade; the result is that the 21st century will inevitably be a world no longer subject to the horrific deterrent logic of Mutually Assured Destruction; under those circumstances, the chances of nuclear war must be quite high if the system is allowed to continue for more than a few decades. If the 20th century witnessed recurrent *barbarity*, barbarism in the full sense of Rosa Luxemburg's use of the term is a very real prospect in the 21st century.

One merit of Hobsbawm's book is that he comes close to recognising this. He concludes:

> We live in a world captured, rooted and upturned by the titanic economic and techno-scientific process of the development of capitalism, which has dominated for the past two or three centuries. We know that it cannot go on as **ad infinitum**. The future cannot be a continuation of the past, and there are signs that we have reached a point of historic crisis. The forces generated by the techno-scientific economy are enough to destroy the environment, that is to say, the material foundations of human life... Our world risks both explosion and implosion. It must change... If humanity is to have a recognisable future, it cannot be by prolonging the past or present... The price of failure, that the alternative to a changed society, is darkness.[10]

But having made the diagnosis, Hobsbawm can offer no cure. His suggestions,[11] made soon after the book was published, amounted to going along with Tony Blair's vision of New Labour, even if he has been slightly more critical since. He can offer no others, because the working class has disappeared from his scheme of things.[12]

Yet the last quarter of the 20th century saw several major states shaken by new upsurges of workers, even if workers did not take advantage of their successes to establish new states acting in their own interests. It was the entry of oil workers into struggles which pulled the carpet from under the Shah's regime in Iran in 1979; it was workers who showed how easy it was to puncture the totalitarian pretensions of the late Stalinist states with the Polish movement of 1980-1981, and it was workers who dealt a death blow against forces looking towards a repressive solution to the problem of these states with the miners' strikes in the Soviet Union in 1989 and 1991; it was workers who shook the French conservative government, with its record parliamentary majority, in November and December 1995. In none of these cases were workers the major beneficiaries of their own actions: in Iran the gainers were the section of the bourgeoisie around Ayatollah Khomeini; in the Eastern bloc those sections of the old ruling class who jumped ship to embrace the market and their own versions of capitalist democracy; in France the rejuvenated social democracy of Jospin. The power the workers deployed was real enough; so too was their ability momentarily to draw behind them all the other discontented and oppressed groups in society. Their weakness was ideological, a willingness to accept definitions of what should be done provided by some of these other groups, especially the radical intelligentsia and disaffected members of the old ruling class. The result was what may be called 'deflected workers' movements'.

Yet the ideological weakness should not surprise anyone with a modicum of knowledge of past class struggles. New classes that emerge with changes in production always start off life by accepting the definitions of society imposed on them by the old order. Their members have never known any other sort of society and take its assumptions for granted. Only as they are driven to struggle by the conditions under which they find themselves do they begin to develop new ways of seeing things, and even then they do not uniformly and immediately reject the old ways. What emerges is what Gramsci called 'contradictory consciousness' or what Lenin, speaking of the Russian working class at the beginning of the 20th century, called 'trade union consciousness'—a defensive challenge to certain aspects of the old society and its ideology, while continuing to accept other aspects. The history of the rise of the bourgeoisie is one of several hundred years of such contradictory conceptions—of on the one hand making wealth in ways very different to the feudal lords and adopting correspondingly new ideas, and on the other wanting to rise within existing society and accepting its old ideas. Such contradictory notions cost the bourgeoise dear in many of its early battles to defend itself as society moved into crisis: its deference to the old order led it to suffer devastating setbacks in places like northern Italy, Germany and France in the 16th and 17th centuries; when it broke through in England in 1649 and France in 1789-1794, it was because a minority emerged within the bourgeoisie which was prepared to work with poorer sections of the middle class to impose its will on the rest as well as on the defenders of the old order.

There is no reason to expect the working class to do what the bourgeoisie never did, and to jump straight to a new, pure and a noncontradictory world view. The history of industrial capitalism so far has been of sections of workers moving in this direction, but then repeatedly being defeated and demoralised, losing faith in their ability to change things. The second quarter of the 20th century saw defeats on a massive scale, with the isolation of the Russian Revolution and the rise of Stalinism in Russia, and then the defeat of the German working class and the conquest of most of mainland Europe by Nazism. The defeats a class suffers can have the effect of bringing on more defeats; people lose faith in their own ability to change things and put their trust in those from other classes who are necessarily going to lead them to more defeats; after the defeat in Germany the most militant workers, desperate for an alternative to Nazism but lacking faith in their own ability to fight successfully, put their faith in Stalinism on the one hand and the 'democratic' bourgeois politicians on the other. This led the great waves of workers struggles, in 1934-1936 and in 1943-1945 into compromise with the system and to defeat.

In the second half of the 20th century another important factor came into play. The very rapidity of growth of the working class in many countries meant there were vast numbers of workers with no historic link to the past. They were the children of peasants, not of previous generations of class conscious workers—and often of peasants living many thousands of miles away. Only a minority of those who occupied the French factories in 1968 were the children of those who had done so in 1936; very few of the Spanish workers who took on Francoism in the mid-1970s had more than tenuous links with the revolutionary anarchosyndicalist and socialist workers of the mid-1930s; virtually none of the Russian miners who were so important in 1989 and 1991 had any connection back to the very much smaller (possibly one tenth the size) working class of 1917. Every lesson had to be learnt over again; it could not all happen in one go. The ideological development of a growing class had to start again near the beginning.

The beginning is not the end. The workers' movements of the last quarter of the 20th century, deflected though they were, were also a foretaste of what we should expect from the larger than ever, more universal than ever working class which enters the new millennium. The most literate, the most cultured, the most homogenous exploited class the world has ever known faces a period every bit as dangerous as Hobsbawm suggests. Where he is wrong in his forecasts is where he is wrong in his history. He does not see that the dynamics of the system itself will force workers to struggle, and that when they struggle they will have the potential to adopt the new world view necessary to lead humanity as whole away from barbarism and towards socialism. Whether this potential is realised cannot be foretold in advance. That depends upon the degree to which the minority of workers and intellectuals who are already won to the new world view are successful in agitating, organising and educating their fellows.

Notes

1   I Berlin, R Dumont and W Golding, quoted at the beginning of E Hobsbawm, *The Age of Extremes* (London, 1994), p1.
2   E Bernstein, *Evolutionary Socialism* (London, 1909), pxi.
3   Ibid, p159.
4   Ibid, p160.
5   See A Crosland, *The Future of Socialism* (London, 1956); J Strachey, *Contemporary Capitalism* (London, 1956); D Bell, *The End of Ideology* (Illinois, 1960)
6   See especially the various editions of her 1898 pamphlet *Reform or Revolution.*
7   See the various editions of her *Junius Pamphlet.*
8   E Hobsbawm, *The Age of Extremes*, op cit, p144.
9   E Hobsbawm, *The Age of Imperialism* (London, 1989), p109.
10   E Hobsbawm, *The Age of Extremes*, op cit, p584-585.
11   In articles in *The Guardian*. See, for instance, 20 June 1996
12   He has insisted, for instance in TV interviews, that while Marx was right about the crisis prone nature of capitalism, he was wrong about the working class.

Is Modernism dead?

*A review of T J Clark, **Farewell to an Idea: Episodes from a History of Modernism** (Yale University Press, 1999), £30*

MIKE GONZALEZ

I will not accept such fitting and fitted. **William Blake**

All art is an attempt to define and make unnatural the distinction between the actual and the desirable. **John Berger**

Tim Clark's contribution to the remaking of art history has been extraordinary. His work on the painting of 19th century France has explored with great sensitivity the struggle that great events set off within artists. What is remarkable in his writing is the combination of an exploration of the painting itself with a microscopic eye and a powerful sense of the great historical forces that invade, in one way or another, even the most secret corners of the canvas. 'The artists that matter come at the facts of politics sideways, unexpectedly, taking themselves by surprise,' Clark says in the conclusion to his brilliant exploration of art and politics in France between 1848 and 1871, *The Absolute Bourgeois* (1973). Its companion work on Courbet, *Image of the People*, written in the same year, is equally as powerful.

The crucial thing about Clark's insight is his insistence that 'the making of a work of art is one historical process among other acts, events and structures'. Art is not autonomous. At one level it is a form of labour, shaped by the prevailing conditions of production, artistic or industrial. At another, Clark insists, it exists in the realm of ideology—it is part of a process of understanding, of making sense of the world. At times it can have a direct political role, subverting and undermining the prevailing ideas. At others it may resonate with fury or despair at its own inability to subvert, especially when, as in the modern age, that act of defiance can so quickly be sabotaged itself by the work of art's conversion into an object of consumption.

So art movements do not have their own history but share the common experience. How they mediate or respond to that is a different issue, of course. Some 25 years after writing those two remarkable books, Clark has published a hugely ambitious overview of Modernism, an attempt to trace—in an avowedly Marxist framework—the fate of art in its conflict with the forces of history. At times, often in fact, artists have taken refuge in the work, in its 'painterly' quality—but was it possible to keep out the noise of the world? Clark's answer until now has always been a definitive no—and that is what has set his work apart.

The Marxist tradition in art criticism is a search for that which is 'fully human' and is denied by a capitalism that fragments and atomises human experience into shards, into individual functions of a hidden machine. That is why we have always argued that capitalism is deeply inimical to art—it may transform it into commodity or consign it to the margins of reason, but it will never answer its questions.

The great art of the 19th century posed its interrogations with a brutal clarity: Delacroix gave freedom flesh and the struggle for it great drama; Courbet invested labour with a power and dignity. But perhaps the art of a confident burgeoning bourgeois society had its more representative expressions in architecture and engineering, at once heroic monuments and practical interventions in the world—bridges, dams, highways, towers. And yet there were insoluble paradoxes, so brilliantly expressed by Marx when he pointed to the monumental solidity that so quickly 'melts into air'.

Out of that paradox, Modernism was born. It ceased to document the world, but we should not make the mistake of imagining that it stopped representing it. Representation, however, is a difficult and slippery notion—how does Jackson Pollock 'represent' anything in his drip paintings? How do Lissitsky's flying wedges or Malevich's black squares picture a real world? Even a work that can apparently be as easily read off the canvas as David's *The Death of Marat* 'represents' a great deal more than a body in a bath.

In the course of his book T J Clark returns to that relationship many times and has a number of stabs at defining it. Indeed, his text is full of caveats and cautions—he has an infuriating habit of inserting brackets in the middle of sentences which contain a single word and a question mark that suggest he is hedging his bets as well as doing that very postmodernist thing of throwing a statement into doubt as soon as it is made.

In the end we can probably agree that a definition of Modernist art work is impossible, and yet most of those who attend exhibitions would feel able to point out the Modernists. They would be the paintings which could not be easily 'read back' into the world, whose subjects could not be traced from the painting to the street. And yet *Guernica* or *The Scream* obviously say something very important to us, just as Van Gogh's Arles paintings said so much about the artist's state of mind, although the subject was trees or cornfields. So there is obviously a relationship with aspects of reality—and a dramatic, deeply sceptical one at that.

The end of the end?

Clark's turning point, or the last 'episode' in this map of what he calls 'Episodes from a History of Modernism', is undoubtedly 1989. His Marxism, with its powerful anarchist impulse, would not have lamented the collapse of Eastern Europe for a moment—indeed he would, at earlier times, have celebrated it as a new beginning. But now he seems to feel it has all come too late. The phrase that recurs throughout is Schiller's: 'the disenchantment of the world'. Art is a struggle against and with that terrible sense of loss, but, although he is ambivalent at the very end, the strong sense from Clark's conclusion is that there is no longer a place from which to imagine the transformation of the world. The transformation of art works into commodities is so rapid, the colonisation of the languages and systems through which the world is described so absolute, that it seems there is little to be done.

It is a familiar argument, and, funnily enough, it arises out of the very thing that Clark rails against most often—'contingency', adaptation to the immediate or what Raymond Williams memorably called 'long term adjustments to short term crises'. And yet if anything gives the lie to such cultural pessimism it is the very 'episodes' recounted in such loving detail in this book. These seven moments in a history of Modernism begin, surprisingly perhaps, with David and *The Death of Marat*. Clark is an absolute master of the art of travelling into and through an art work (in particular, in my view, when he discusses Picasso and Pollock). It seems at first sight to be a very early place to start, except that the key to Modernism, as far as this writer is concerned, is its absolutely central grasp of the contradictions of economic progress under capitalism. 'Modernity', the development of industry, the evolution of the commodity, the forging of a fully fledged proletariat, is both a creative and a destructive process. That was at the core of Marx's understanding of capitalism's unfolding. Equally, art has provided a space where those contradictions have been explored. So Modernism is born with—but not out of—the construction of a modern economy. Clark finds the impulse to capitalist modernisation enough to produce the Modernist question.

There is in all of these key works of Modernism a struggle between the demands of the moment ('contingency') and a vision of the future, an 'imaginative possibility of social revolution' (as a more modern critic, Perry Anderson, put it). It is a well trodden argument that art suggests universals—moral, philosophical, religious at different times—whereas the restless materialism of the modern age dispenses with such things. 'Modernism turns on the impossibility of transcendence,' Clark says— and should have added, to explain the nearly 400 pages that follow, 'but refuses to accept that impossibility.' So, in his exploration of *Marat*, Clark finds a David whose dead revolutionary is caught in a moment of writing (he holds a letter). The empty upper half of the painting is full of possibility. The suggestion is that this work is not, as so many others were, designed to freeze the image of Marat into a symbol of the French Revolution (as David himself did elsewhere), but rather to disengage the qualities of a revolutionary leader from that particular life, that particular body. So even now, the argument is about what Marat represents, rather than what he was or is.

The long chapter that follows centres on Pissaro's *We Field-Women*. Clark's discussion ranges eloquently across the canvas and across the historical moment. He moves without effort through politics, music, art and architecture, and sometimes, I have to admit, loses me in the complexities of his argument. But at heart, the same issue arises in 1891 as in 1791. In 'showing' agricultural labour, Pissaro was raising questions of morality, of the relations between human beings and nature. The material meets the moral in the painting, and the idea seeks its expression on the canvas. The problem here, and with greater and greater intensity later, is that the work is an object, a thing in space and time, however much it might wish to be something else. Clark returns to this difficult issue again and again—that art can never throw off its 'thing-ness', and thus its capacity for transformation into a commodity. So, like it or not, the idea expressed in this way is always material, and the withdrawal into the painting can never be complete. That does not undermine the enterprise, but it absolutely guarantees a continuing and unresolved struggle.

In 1891, Clark suggests, a burgeoning modernity was producing a moral crisis of extraordinary depth. This was a turning point, and Pissaro's anarchist allegiances made him, in the writer's view, sensitive to and aware of the depth and nature of it. Van Gogh's first major exhibition, the rediscovery of Monet, the authority of Cézanne, all pointed to a moment in which art was fleeing to the margins and expressing from there its revulsion at the impact of the modern—from Baudelaire's poem *Le Voyage* to *The Scream* is a distance of several decades, but only a single step, I think. Simmel expressed it thus in 1902:

> *The modern mind has become more and more calculating. The calculative*
> *excesses of practical life which the money economy has brought about corre-*
> *spond to the ideal of natural science to transform the world into an arithmetic*
> *problem, to fix every part of the world by mathematical formulas... It is deci-*
> *sive that city life has transformed the struggle with nature for livelihood into*
> *an inter-human struggle for gain, which here is not granted by nature but by*
> *other men.*

In revolt against that 'calculative excess', Cézanne and Picasso provide two different forms of response. Both move away from narrative, from 'representing the real'. It could be said that that particular task had become redundant anyway with the advent of photography, but that is far too simple an explanation. After all, we now know that even the earliest photographers used their plates in a painterly way, or played with the 'reality effect' to make convincing documents of, say, fairies at the bottom of the garden—so the ironising of photography is not such a postmodern business, after all. Clark's journey through Cézanne's various 'Bathers' paintings (1904-1906) is confident and compelling. What emerges is how unstable or mobile the figures are. Homing in on the detail of a sexually indeterminate body in one canvas, it becomes clear that the body has both sets of sexual organs, but depicted with a kind of rush, or even an uncertainty, that makes identity a shifting and uncertain thing. In another moment of the painting, two bodies are fused into one. The landscapes, backgrounds, skies are almost flippantly artificial; all of this is a dream, a metaphor, an assertion of some other place, Cézanne struggling with the visual and symbolic language of his time. The last part of the Cézanne chapter is, I feel, evasive—at least, it is very hard to pin down. But, as I understand it through the earlier examination of the paintings, Cézanne is pursuing a picture of another, possible, world with the materials of this one. He exposes their limits, but does not and probably cannot find another vocabulary to replace it.

Flattening the ground

It is agreed by most critics that Cubism is at the centre of Modernist art, because it asserts a new and different kind of order. In his still brilliant essay 'The Moment of Cubism' John Berger explains that 'Cubism changed the nature of the relationship between the painted image and reality and by doing so expressed a new relationship between man and reality.' Its moment was 'a moment when the promises of the future were more substantial than the present'. Clark puts it in rather more complex ways, as ever, but there is no disagreement as to the extraordinary significance of the years from 1906 to 1910. In his immediately prior work, the *Demoiselles d'Avignon*, Picasso tried to repaint Velázquez, to rescue something from the classical tradition. He toyed with 'primitive alternatives'—African masks or the paintings of the Douanier Rousseau—perhaps in search of a metaphorical language that could speak of an imagined otherness. But while they could critically reflect on the 'modern', they were not of it. And then came Cubism. Faced with that 'disenchantment', Cubism set out to 're-enchant', which meant imagining wholly different relations. Berger sees the great Cubist paintings as diagrams, sketches of a possibility. Clark travels through the spaces and lines of Picasso's paintings of the time, but bumps each time into a surface which resists all attempts to find other depths beneath it. The language of the painting is all there is, is everything. As the Malevich circle in the Russia of 1920 would rediscover, the new art is architecture, experiment in space and form. To return to Berger, it is about relationships and possibilities. *The Guitarist* of 1910, for example, is analogous to the world at the top and bottom of the oval frame, but in between there is a shifting and experimentation, a playing with surface, line and volume. Is this revolutionary? Yes, because it suggests restless change, variety, possibilities still unimagined. Is it Modernist? Yes, in its severance with the past (or its overcoming of the past) and its projection of a visual utopia that prefigures different ways of living to match the different ways of seeing.

Clark is less confident, I believe, though his assumption throughout is that Modernism has an inextricable relationship with utopia and revolutionary thought. His unease, and I suppose that this anticipates his conclusion, is that reality drags the dreamer back to the horror of the present. The First World War threw horror upon horror against the dreamers. It proved beyond any doubt the savagery upon which capitalism rested, but it also engulfed everything and destroyed all morality, and the prophecy at the heart of Cubism seemed to sink without trace in Flanders' fields.

And then came 1917. Clark chooses to address the revolution in art that accompanied the Russian Revolution from the perspective of 1920 and War Communism. Perhaps, as he suggests, it was a key moment in the work of UNOVIS, the movement led by Malevich and represented most familiarly by El Lissitsky's ubiquitous *Flying Red Wedge*. But perhaps there is another reason, to do with Clark's own resolute hostility to Leninism. Curiously this moment of what he calles 'the absolute zero of all indices', an unimaginable social and economic catastrophe imposed by conscious will on the nascent Soviet Republic, was a high point in the process of 'imagining otherwise' so central to the Modernist enterprise. It was, in Clark's words, 'both apocalypse and utopia'. In his view, the commitment to industrialisation and modernisation necessarily carried that 'calculation and contingency' which was always the enemy of dreaming. It was in a sense much simpler than that—necessity stood over Soviet Russia with dripping fangs. Clark recognises how little choice there was, but also underlines the barbarity of it. The paradox is that at this very time what was mobilised by the new republic was a new language, vital and fluid, precisely because in this time of constant convolution nothing remained standing.

What could be the relationship between a disintegrating working class, a siege on every side by well fed armies and the struggle to lift agricultural production, and these odd, sometimes whimsical encounters of squares and circles by Lissitsky, or the black square and the void within it that symbolised the Suprematist movement that Malevich led? In a sense, they picked up again from Cubism. The prophetic impulse lost in the carnage of the First World War was rediscovered with 1917. Gabo's Constructivist manifesto said, 'Nothing is unreal in art. Whatever is touched by art becomes reality, and we do not need to undertake remote and distant navigations in the subconscious in order to reveal a world which lies in our immediate vicinity.' Lissitsky and Malevich called it 'architecture'—the geometries of this new imagined world could become speakers' platforms or housing complexes or advertisements for galoshes. Quite rightly, Clark singles out Lissitsky's design for a monument to Rosa Luxemburg, a familiar arrangement of squares and circles through which, barely glimpsed but pulsating through colour, is the name of Rosa Luxemburg—the future floating beneath the surfaces of the present.

For Clark there is little doubt that Jackson Pollock's extraordinary creations are a limit-case. He represents, at a social level, the most extreme marginalisation of the artist. The many photographs of Pollock in his studio and Namuth's film of Pollock at work show him embedded in a world entirely built of paintings in which he works with a kind of madness. He is the confirmation of how the bourgeoisie sees the artist, and the expression of the way in which that world has driven artists to the very edges of the social world—an act of rejection and refusal on their part that has become a kind of exile. Is it accidental that Pollock's drip paintings suggest imploding dark stars, the line between the world and the void, the known and the unknown? Is it any wonder, too, that they are so obviously angry and aggressive?

For Clark, what drives Modernism is the need to explore the unknowable, with its concomitant refusal to accept that what is is all there is. There is an argument that sees the development of Modernism as a process towards formalism, towards the exploration of pure form. Malevich's 'White on White' paintings might, at first sight, seem to justify that conclusion, until (as Clark shows so convincingly) you approach them and see their movement, their displacement of the eye, their assertion that within an apparent one dimensional reality there are many other lines, dimensions and masses. There is certainly a journey into form as a metaphor, a search for other complex totalities. There is also perhaps an attempt to disengage that experiment from the demands of the material world, but that of course is impossible, partly because the painting is a material thing (which is why it can be commodified) and partly because it has meaning only when it is seen from a place within the world. So Pollock's *Starburst* meets the edges of the canvas, and though his canvases grow bigger, they can never lose their edges.

'There is a line of art stretching back to David and Shelley that makes no sense without its practitioners believing what they did was to resist or exceed the normal understandings of the culture, and that those understandings were their enemy. This is the line of art we call Modernist,' writes Clark. This leads this modern art to challenge and refuse, to look inward and look outward, to reshape nature and to attempt metaphors of different systems of living and believing.

The suggestion in the title of this book and in its maddeningly ambiguous conclusion is that this charge has finally been lost in a world of immediate incorporation and the loss of utopia. And there is undoubtedly some art which is only decoration, a comfortable reaffirmation of all that is as it is. But the rage around the Turner exhibitions suggests that discomfort and offence is still provoked by what is being produced. I have heard Gilbert and George arguing against a Paisleyite vicar who wanted their exhibition banned because it would corrupt and deprave. It turned out that he had never seen a Gilbert and George exhibition—it was the fear of art he expressed. The curious thing is that whenever social struggles arise, they produce an art which is their vision of the world they are struggling for. Tim Clark himself is a product of the generation that lifted the cobbles of the Paris streets and found the beach beneath. Graffiti, like them or not, have become the utopian architecture of the inner city. And so on and on. Art remains a place of struggle, of contradiction. Of course a late capitalism will try to turn everything—even the imagery of revolution—into an object for sale and consumption. That is the manner of its appropriation of all human creativity. But if it momentarily silences the signs of contradiction, it can never hide the paradox and the conflict at its very heart. And with each discovery of that reality will come an impulse to imagine this horror otherwise.

The man behind the mask

*A review of Francis Wheen, **Karl Marx** (Fourth Estate, 1999), £20*

PETER MORGAN

'Above all a revolutionary'

When Frederick Engels spoke at the graveside of his dear friend and
political ally Karl Marx in 1883, he said:

> *It is impossible to measure the loss which the fighting European and
> American proletariat and historical science has lost with the death of this
> man... For Marx was above all a revolutionary, and his great aim in life was
> to co-operate in this or that fashion in the overthrow of capitalist society and
> the state institutions it had created, to co-operate in the emancipation of the
> modern proletariat.*

It is no easy task to write a biography of someone who has been
described as the greatest thinker of the millennium. It is even harder
when the subject is Marx, a man who has been vilified and attacked since
the day he died. Yet Francis Wheen has done justice to his subject. He
has written a compelling, refreshing and honest account of the founder of
modern scientific socialism. Wheen says in his introduction that he has
been keen to write a book about Marx and not about Marxism. 'It is
time', he says, 'to strip away the mythology and try to rediscover Karl
Marx the man.' It is to his credit, therefore, that Wheen has been able to
capture some of that fighting spirit of which Engels spoke and give a
taste of Marx's intellectual stature. He has given a warts and all account

of the life of Marx, which is made all the more candid because he has delved into the masses of letters and correspondence between Marx, Engels and his many other friends and political allies. Wheen has removed many of the myths that have distorted Marx's ideas to give them relevance to those struggling to change the world today. I want to pick some examples of the way he has done this in this brief review of the book.

'Only now do I know what real unhappiness is. I feel broken down...'

The great strength of Wheen's book, and what strikes the reader immediately, is that he shows the human side of Marx. Over the years this has often been overlooked—many people did not realise that beneath the great theoretician there was also a passionate polemicist and organiser, and a man who was caring to his family and loyal to his friends.

Nothing illustrates the human side of Marx better than the tragic case of his youngest son, Edgar. Marx adored his young son. Edgar was always in fine spirits and ready to amuse his family: 'When his parents lapsed into despondency, he could always cheer them up by singing nonsensical ditties—or the Marseillaise, for that matter—with tremendous feeling and at the top of his voice'.[1] So when he was laid low with a gastric fever there was much concern in the Marx household. Although he recovered temporarily, his remission was short lived. He eventually took a turn for the worse, and a doctor diagnosed that there would be no hope of recovery. On 6 April 1855 he died in his father's arms shortly before six in the morning.

The death of Marx's dear son 'shattered him to the core'. It was the third time one of Marx's children had died, but for Karl this was the most painful. The funeral of Edgar took place at the Whitfield Tabernacle in Tottenham Court Road, which was also the resting place for the two other children. One of the few things that kept Marx going and that sustained him over the coming months was his close friendship to Engels. The Marx family suffered in many other ways. They faced terrible poverty and destitution. The bailiffs were constantly on their doorstep and the police spies were always on the prowl. In the face of such harassment it is amazing that Marx survived, and survived with enough energy to make an enormous contribution to the socialist movement.

But although Wheen recalls the bad and difficult times, and there were many, he also tells of the good times. We read of Marx's loving relationship with Jenny von Westphalen, his childhood sweetheart from Trier; his rowdy student days; his drunken pub crawls with friends up and down Tottenham Court Road which ended with them being chased by the police; his all night chess games with his friend Wilhelm

Liebknecht (for chess buffs, one of the games is printed in the appendix); and the many Sundays spent on Hampstead Heath with children and friends. There is much here to reveal what Marx was like and what sustained him when things were hard.

Wheen also reveals the experiences which helped feed Marx's genius. Marx led an extraordinary life, partly because he lived through such extraordinary times. He experienced the revolutions of 1848 and the strike wave of 1868-1869, and observed the Paris Commune of 1871. He contributed to, and edited, radical newspapers. He was a pamphleteer, an agitator and an organiser. He was central to the first workers' associations that were formed to support the growing workers' movement throughout Europe, and all the time he was a most prolific writer. His collected works extend to over 50 volumes, and his ideas have transformed the way we see the world and the way we go about changing it. Marx was a revolutionary, not just in what he wrote, but in what he did. Bringing this side of Marx to life is one of the book's strengths. And at the young age of 30 he found out what revolution was all about.

'Our age, the age of democracy, is breaking...'

So wrote an ecstatic Frederick Engels as revolution swept Europe in 1848. Engels and Marx had just completed their great pamphlet *The Communist Manifesto*. But, by the time it appeared, revolution had spread throughout Europe—in Palermo in January; in Paris in February; and in Berlin, Vienna, Budapest, Prague and Milan by the end of March. Barricades were set up. Workers took over the streets, and were even in the government in Paris. The sense of euphoria was everywhere, and it seemed that the old system was collapsing under the weight of popular uprisings.

Nowhere was this more true than in Germany. Compared to its western neighbours, Germany was still quite a backward country. It was dominated by agricultural production. German cities had grown little since the 16th century, German political structures were backward and Germany was still divided between 39 states. The demand for national unification was of central importance to all progressive democrats.

Two young German revolutionaries recognised this as the uprising they had been waiting for. Marx and Engels hurried back to their native Rhineland to intervene in the struggle. By May they had arrived in Cologne and founded the radical daily paper *Neue Rheinische Zeitung*. In a short time it was selling 5,000 copies a day, a huge circulation by the standards of the time. Its intention was to spread the revolution and to argue the case for the most left wing revolutionary course.

But such was the backwardness of German society and so timid was the German bourgeoisie that at every step it would rather compromise with the old order than align itself with the more radical elements that wanted to take the movement forward. The result was that by the end of 1848 the great revolutionary wave that had swept Germany went down to defeat and the old order was able to survive. The regime then took retribution against those who had fought against it. At the beginning of 1849 Karl Marx and Frederick Engels stood trial for insulting the public prosecutor. In an appeal to the jurors' political conscience Marx declared:

> *I prefer to follow the great events of the world, to analyse the course of history, than to occupy myself with local bosses, with the police and prosecuting magistrates. However great these gentlemen may imagine themselves in their own fancy, they are **nothing** in the gigantic battles of the present time. I consider we are making a real sacrifice when we decide to break a lance with these opponents. But, firstly, it is the duty of the press to come forward on behalf of the oppressed in its immediate neighbourhood...the first duty of the press now is to **undermine all the foundations of the existing political state of affairs**.*[2]

There followed a period of loud applause from the crowded courtroom, and Marx and Engels were subsequently acquitted. The prosecution came back for more. The very next day Marx found himself in the dock, this time with two colleagues from the Rhenish District Committee of Democrats. Their crime was incitement to revolt. Considering that revolution was the order of the day, it would have been unusual for Marx not to be urging resistance against the old order. But once again, after an appeal to the jury, Marx and his colleagues were unanimously acquitted. In the words of one liberal weekly paper, 'In political trials the government nowadays has no luck at all with the juries.'

The government decided that the only way to deal with the impetuous Marx was to kick him out of the country. On 16 May 1849 the authorities prosecuted half the editorial staff of the *Neue Rheinische Zeitung* and recommended the other half for deportation. The final issue of the paper was defiantly printed in red ink, with the editors announcing, 'Their last word everywhere and always will be: emancipation of the working class.' And with a band playing and a red flag flying from the rooftops, Marx and his fellow journalists marched out of the building, whereupon Marx fled to Paris, and then on to London, where he was to spend the rest of his life in exile.

Marx's role in the revolution which swept Europe in 1848 and his analysis of what happened, in his book *The 18th Brumaire of Louis*

Bonaparte, revealed his true greatness, as it did that of his closest friend Frederick Engels.

'Ten days that shook the world'

The phrase may be from John Reed's book on the Russian Revolution, but Francis Wheen uses it to describe the first meeting between Marx and Engels in 1844, which also lasted for ten days. Engels said some 40 years later, 'When I visited Marx in Paris in the summer of 1844, our complete agreement in all theoretical fields became evident and our joint work dates from that time.' By the time of this first meeting Engels was already a political theorist in his own right. Initially Marx was suspicious of Engels—he came from Berlin and Marx thought he was still heavily influenced by idealist German philosophy. But this suspicion quickly disappeared after Marx read Engels' essays on political economy which he had written for a German newspaper. They were, declared Marx, a work of genius. Partly this impact arose from Marx's lack of knowledge about political economy, as Wheen explains:

> *Though he had already decided that abstract idealism was so much hot air, and that the engine of history was driven by economic and social forces, Marx's practical knowledge of capitalism was nil. He had been so engaged by his dialectical tussle with German philosophers that the condition of England—the first industrialised country, the birthplace of the proletariat—had escaped his notice. Engels, from his vantage point in the cotton mills of Lancashire, was well placed to enlighten him.*[3]

Engels had moved to Manchester in 1842 to work at the family firm, Ermen and Engels. At the time Manchester was the centre of the 1842 general strike and a city teeming with Chartists and industrial agitators. The book Engels wrote at this time—*The Condition of the Working Class in England*—remains, even today, one of the great studies of industrial capitalism:

> *What gave the book its power and depth was Engels' skilful interweaving (he was a textile man, after all) of first hand observation with information from parliamentary commissions, health officials and copies of Hansard. The British state may have done little or nothing to improve the lot of the workers, but it had collected a mass of data about the horrors of industrial life which was available to anyone who cared to retrieve it from the dusty library shelf... After quoting several gruesome cases of disease and starvation, published in the middle class **Manchester Guardian**, [Engels] exulted: 'I delight in the testimony of my opponents'. One need only study the citations from government*

Blue Books and the **Economist** *in the first volume of* **Capital** *to see how much
Karl Marx learned from the technique.*[4]

And yet Engels was keen to defer to the genius of Marx from the
outset. He accepted that it was his duty to support and subsidise Marx
without complaint but Wheen is right to recognise the contribution that
Engels made to Marx, not just in terms of financial and moral support,
but also intellectually. Engels was instrumental in the content of *The
Communist Manifesto*. The *Manifesto* was commissioned by the
Communist League—a grouping of radicals and workers committed to
revolutionary communism—in 1847 as a 'profession of faith'. Engels
wrote an early draft in June 1847, which he then sent on to Marx.

Marx was keen that *The Communist Manifesto* be an open statement
about the aims and intentions of communists. He wanted to break out of
the conspiratorial tradition that dominated radical groups at the time.
Why, he wanted to know, should revolutionaries hide their views and
intentions? When the two men met at the end of November 1847 at
Ostend en route to London for the second congress of the Communist
League, Engels had revised his original draft. But even so, both he and
Marx realised they had a fight on their hands to get it accepted by the
delegates.

The venue for the second congress was a room above the Red Lion
pub in Great Windmill Street, Soho. Marx and Engels submitted their
proposals, and then a bitter and prolonged debate raged for ten days.
Eventually Marx and Engels carried the congress with them, and they
were given the job of writing the *Manifesto* in the name of the League.

The contrast between the June congress and that of November
showed the extent to which Marx and Engels shifted the revolutionaries
to a much sharper and harder analysis of capitalism. At the June congress
(which Marx had not attended) the League's aims were declared as 'the
emancipation of humanity by spreading the theory of the community or
property and its speediest possible practical introduction'. By November
the rules were much more combative: 'The aim of the League is the
overthrow of the bourgeoisie, the rule of the proletariat, the abolition of
the old bourgeois society which rests on the antagonism of classes, and
without private property'.[5] Engels' ideas were important, but in the end
Marx wrote the final *Manifesto*.

There was much else besides that Engels contributed to Marx. After
the Communist League was dissolved in 1852, Marx was commissioned
to write a series of articles for the weekly *New York Tribune*—a huge
and influential paper with a readership of 200,000. A series of articles
called 'Revolution and Counter-Revolution in Germany' appeared in 19
instalments between October 1851 and October 1852 with Marx's by-
line. In fact it was wholly written by Engels. Such was Engels' military

understanding that, when he wrote anonymously on the progress of the Russo-Turkish war in 1853, rumour and gossip attributed it to an American general. And when Marx was commissioned to write entries on great generals and the history of warfare for a friend who was compiling entries for a new encyclopaedia, he happily accepted $2 per page and then got Engels to do all the work for him.

Their relationship suffered only one serious setback. On 7 January 1863 Engels wrote to Marx and informed him of the death of his partner, Mary Burns. The response from Marx hurt Engels immensely. Marx went on about his poor financial position, the problems with paying school fees for the kids and the difficulty of working. Engels was amazed, angered and hurt. It took a couple of weeks, and an apology (of sorts) from Marx, before friendly relations were restored. There is little than can be said in mitigation for Marx and, quite rightly, Wheen doesn't try—there is no doubt that Marx was seriously out of order. But it was the only rift in what was a remarkable friendship, quickly forgotten and never mentioned again.

'I simply cannot understand', wrote Engels in 1881, nearly 40 years after first meeting Marx, 'how anyone can be envious of genius; it's something so very special that we who have not got it know it to be unattainable right from the start.' As Francis Wheen acknowledges, for Engels, 'Marx's friendship, and the triumphant culmination of his work, would be reward enough'.[6]

'What resilience, what historical initiative, what a capacity for sacrifice in these Parisians'

There was no controlling Marx's excitement at the events in France's capital city on 18 March 1871, as workers established the Paris Commune. Of the 92 communards elected by popular suffrage on 28 March, 17 were members of the International Working Men's Association (First International)—the group that had been set up in September 1864 to further the cause of workers' revolt, and which had Marx as one of its guiding figures. The central role that Marx played in the Association blows a hole in one of the most popular myths about him—that he was an intellectual interested only in studying books. In fact, as Francis Wheen shows, Marx's role in the Association demonstrates the coming together of his revolutionary politics with his revolutionary activity.

Marx himself wrote about the Paris Commune for the General Council of the Association in the extraordinary pamphlet *The Civil War in France*. But it did not appear until after the Commune had been drowned in blood. Why the delay? For some biographers, this delay is attributed to Marx's personal ambivalence. But as Wheen demonstrates,the delay was much more due to mundane and routine reasons—at the time Marx suffered bronchitis and liver trouble that prevented him from writing. When it did appear, *The Civil War in France* was a brilliant analysis of what the Commune had achieved—demonstrating for the first time what form workers' power would take. The pamphlet was an immediate success. The first two printings of 3,000 each sold out within a fortnight. When it became known that Marx was the author he rapidly became notorious, and so too did the Association, which became the subject of a witch hunt.

The response of those in positions of power 'who can never believe that ordinary people might be able or willing to challenge them' is to hunt for the 'trouble makers', as Wheen says: 'whether a single Mr Big or a "tightly knit group of politically motivated men" that has been pulling the strings'.[7] Yet in defending the role of the Association in the uprising of Parisian workers, Marx knew of only one response to such intimidation:

> *Our Association is, in fact, nothing but the international bond between the most advanced working men in the various countries of the civilised world. Wherever, in whatever shape, and under whatever conditions the class struggle obtains any consistency, it is but natural that members of our Association should stand in the foreground.*[8]

The movement in France was effectively smashed and the Association was weakened. The French section was outlawed, the German section faced heavy repression, and in Britain two of the trade union leaders who were on the General Council resigned to join Gladstone's Liberal Party. The Association was dying, but for Marx there was another problem to deal with—that of the anarchist Michael Bakunin, who was threatening to take over the Association from within.

Bakunin was a romantic revolutionist and conspirator with a rather confused anti-authoritarian programme. He is often described as the father of modern anarchism, although, as Wheen notes, 'he bequeathed no great theoretical scripture'. Wheen then proceeds to demolish the arguments of those, such as Isaiah Berlin, who imply that Bakunin was some kind of free thinker and libertarian spirit whereas Marx was just a dogmatic and literal minded plodder.

Bakunin's International Alliance of Socialist Democracy had entered the Association in 1868. This prompted a vicious faction fight that went on for the next four years between Marx and the General Council on the one hand and Bakunin and his supporters on the other. When the struggle in Europe was at its peak the faction fight was of less importance. Once it went down to defeat, however, Bakunin saw his chance. In this situation

Marx and Engels had only one option. At the Hague congress that Marx attended in person both he and Engels succeeded in winning the majority of delegates to have Bakunin expelled. But, fearful that Bakunin might make a comeback and take over the organisation that had clearly had its day, Engels proposed that the Association be moved to New York, a motion that was narrowly passed by the delegates.

Engels later described the First International as the force in European history on whose side the future lay. And he was to be proved correct. Half a century later Lenin and Trotsky looked back at the Paris Commune and the role of the International, and they used *The Civil War in France* as the blueprint for the 1917 Russian Revolution.

'So, this volume is finished. I owe it to you alone that it was possible...'

In the early hours of 16 August 1867 Marx finished revising and correcting the proofs of his greatest work, *Capital*. In a letter to Engels he praised the sacrifice his friend had made for him: 'Without your self sacrifice for me I could not possibly have managed the immense labour demanded by the three volumes. I embrace you full of thanks... Salut, my dear, valued, friend'.[9]

While completing the last pages Marx was in considerable pain. For years he had suffered a whole host of physical illnesses, in particular the carbuncles that regularly afflicted him. Through the winter of 1866-1867, however, they could no longer thwart his determination to finish his great work. As Wheen explains, 'He wrote the last few pages of volume one standing at his desk when an eruption of boils around the rump made sitting too painful... Engels' experienced eye immediately spotted certain passages in the text "where the carbuncles have left their mark", and Marx agreed that the fever in his groin might have given the prose a rather livid hue. "At all events, I hope the bourgeoisie will remember the carbuncles until their dying day", he cursed. "What a swine they are!"'[10]

But despite the physical problems, Marx produced a book of such immense power and influence that Engels later described it as 'the bible of the working class'. Wheen launches an admirable defence of *Capital*. He attacks the philosopher Karl Popper, who claims that Marx's economic laws are nothing other than historical prophesies. In fact, says Wheen, 'it would be easy to subject Marx's economic assertions to...experiment by studying what has happened in practice during the last century or so. As capitalism matured, he predicted, we would see periodic recessions, an ever growing dependence on technology and the growth of huge, quasi-monopolistic corporations spreading their sticky tentacles all over the world in search of new markets to exploit. If none of this had happened, we might be forced to agree that the old boy was talking poppycock'.[11] He also defends Marx from those who claim that, because workers have not got progressively poorer since the early days of capitalism, this somehow disproves the theory. 'What Marx did predict', argues Wheen, 'was that under capitalism there would be a *relative*—not an absolute—decline in wages'.[12] And finally he attacks Leszek Kolakowski, who claims that 'Marx's theory of value does not meet the normal requirements of a scientific hypothesis, especially that of falsiability.' Unfortunately Wheen's defence of *Capital* is weakened by the fact that he compares it to 'a Victorian melodrama or a vast gothic novel', rather than in appreciating the real scientific breakthrough that Marx achieved. But his admiration for the great work shines through.

Sometimes Wheen's attempt to explain some of the Marx's ideas lead to him trivialising them. His explanation of the dialectic—which was so crucial to Marx's early intellectual development and, later, to his writings on economics—is too simplified to be convincing. But, at the same time, Wheen is not scared to take up some of the arguments and some of the theoretical questions that have dogged studies of Marx for many years. For example, there has been a debate in the history of Marxism about whether there is a sharp break between the young Marx and the old Marx. The old Marx, it has been claimed, was the scientific and economistic Marx, whereas the early one was the idealist philosopher. What is Wheen's conclusion? He makes this tongue-in-cheek comment: 'Wine may mature and improve in the bottle, but it remains wine for all that.' But then he does go on to describe the *Grundisse* (1857-1858)—Marx's fragmentary compilation of notes which look at alienation, dialectics, labour power and surplus value, and which anticipated the later writings in *Capital*—as the missing link between the *Economic and Philosophical Manuscripts* (1844) and *Capital* (1867). His argument is not wholly conclusive, but he does come down on the right side.

This is a book, though, that once you start reading you don't want to put down. Finishing Wheen's *Karl Marx* gives the reader an immediate desire to want to know more. Many readers of this book will be hungry to learn more about the life and revolutionary ideas of Karl Marx. They will want to read *Capital* for the first time, or read it again. They will want to remember the excitement of the Paris Commune in the pages of *The Civil War in France*. Above all, for many there will be a burning desire to follow in the footsteps of this great revolutionary and finish off the great task that Marx set himself—the overthrow of capitalism. That is no bad thing.

Notes

1   F Wheen, *Karl Marx* (Fourth Estate, 1999), p216.
2   Quoted ibid, p143.
3   Ibid, p75.
4   Ibid, pp82-83.
5   Ibid, p118.
6   Ibid, pp83-84.
7   Ibid, pp330-331.
8   Ibid, p331.
9   Ibid, p298.
10   Ibid, p294.
11   Ibid, p299.
12   Ibid, p300.

The Far Left in the English Revolution

BRIAN MANNING

BRIAN MANNING is one of the foremost historians of the English Revolution. He has defended and extended an explicitly Marxist approach to history. In his latest book he examines the role of the most radical elements within the English Revolution, which he controversially calls the far left. He demonstrates that this far left foreshadowed the development of working class consciousness and revolutionary socialist politics. This fascinating volume is essential reading for all those who wish to find out about the extraordinary political developments in this most exciting period in English history.

The Far Left in the English Revolution 1640 to 1660

BRIAN MANNING

All power to the imagination

A review of Marshall Berman, **Adventures in Marxism** *(Verso, 1999), £17*

ANNE ALEXANDER

Why is it that civilised humanity
Can make the world so wrong?
In this hurly burly of insanity,
Our dreams cannot last long.
We've reached a deadline,
A press headline,
Every sorrow,
Blues value, is news value tomorrow.
Blues, 20th century blues,
Are getting me down,
Who's escaped those weary,
20th century blues?

At the end of the 1990s it seems that few of us can escape the grip of Noel Coward's '20th Century Blues'. So much of our society seems fragmented, distorted and confused. War, economic crisis and revolution have all knocked the self confidence out of early 20th century predictions of progress. For many commentators this chaos can never be fully explained, and any attempt to change it by conscious human action is naive folly. It appears that, as Francis Fukyama said, 'the 20th century has made all of us into deep historical pessimists'.[1]

Marshall Berman, however, has never been a pessimist, as this collection of essays shows. Whether he is writing about Marx, describing 'Georg

Lukács' Cosmic Chutzpah', or simply sketching a pen portrait of one of
his students, Berman always tries to get beneath the surface to understand
the deeper forces which shape our lives. For him, seeking some meaning
from the maelstrom of modern life has never been a futile exercise. Using
Marx's ideas, he attempts to trace the currents guiding the torrent of new
ideas, social structures, political organisations, economic forms and artistic
innovations thrown up by capitalist society. From the moment he first
picked up a copy of Marx's *Economic and Philosophical Manuscripts*[2] in
the Soviet Four Continents bookstore in New York, to the present day, he
has lost nothing of his sense of exhilaration at finding the intellectual tools
to help him do this:

> *The staff knew just what book I wanted: Marx's **Economic and Philosophical***
> ***Manuscripts of 1844**... I opened it at random, here, there, somewhere else—*
> *and suddenly I was in a sweat, melting, shedding clothes and tears, flashing*
> *hot and cold. I rushed to the front: 'I've got to have this book!'*[3]

Berman's writing is infused with a sense of deep personal involvement with the ideas and people he meets during his 'adventures in
Marxism'. His urgent need to communicate his passion for Marx's
writing characterises each of the essays in this collection. Just as urgent
is his desire to rescue Marx from those who want to lock his ideas away
behind dogma, academic mystification and hostile polemic. He gave
away the copies of Marx's *Economic and Philosophical Manuscripts*
indiscriminately to bewildered relatives, friends and acquaintances.

Faced with two sterile versions of Marxism—one the stuff of Stalinist
dogma, the other drawn from Cold War caricatures—he seized on the
Economic and Philosophical Manuscripts as the starting point for a new
kind of Marxism, one which celebrated Marx's individualism, his
passion and his rebellion, against the monoliths of the 1950s:

> *'Let me get this straight,' my mother said, as she took her book. 'It's Marx,*
> *but not communism, right? So what is it?'... I felt like a panellist on a TV quiz*
> *show, with time running out. I reached for a phrase I had seen in **The New***
> ***York Times**, in a story about French existentialists—Sartre, De Beauvoir,*
> *Henri Lefebrve, Andre Gorcz, and their friends—who were trying to merge*
> *their thought with Marxism and create a radical perspective that would tran-*
> *scend the dualisms of the Cold War. I said, 'Call it Marxist humanism'.*[4]

A decade after the fall of the Berlin Wall, and eight years on from the
collapse of the Soviet Union, it is hard to imagine the sense of challenge
that the phrase 'Marxist humanism'encapsulated in the 1950s. In Europe
and the US a growing number of people were becoming disenchanted

with the monolithic Stalinist Communist parties. In France, Britain and
the US small groups of intellectuals began to form around a common
rejection of Stalinism. They were only loosely organised through discussion circles and critical journals, but the sense of a movement
crystallised around the ideas of 'Marxist humanism' and the name the
'New Left'.

For the New Left, Stalinism turned Marx's ideas into rigid dogma, as
oblivious to human action as the laws of physics. As one of the characters in Jean-Paul Sartre's novel *Iron in the Soul* tries patiently to explain
to a doubter:

> *It is conceivable that the Politburo might founder in the depths of stupidity:*
> *by the same token it is conceivable that the roof of this hut might fall on your*
> *head, but that doesn't mean you spend your time keeping a wary eye on the*
> *ceiling.*[5]

The critical event which propelled a whole generation of left wing
intellectuals away from the dead embrace of the Communist parties was
the Hungarian Revolution. As Russian tanks rolled into Budapest to
crush a workers' uprising, figures such as Edward and Dorothy
Thompson, John Saville and Christopher Hill left the Communist Party
of Great Britain in protest. Thompson and Saville made an explicit
attempt to link Marxism and humanism in the first editorial of their new
discussion journal, *The New Reasoner*, in July 1956:

> *History has provided a chance for* [a] *re-examination* [of Marxism-Leninism]
> *to take place; and for the scientific methods of Marxism to be integrated with*
> *the finest traditions of the human reason and spirit which we may best*
> *describe as humanism.*[6]

Against the might of Soviet Marxology, with its institute in Moscow
and its ranks of experts, the intellectual rebels of the New Left took up
the writings of 'the young Marx'. Berman argues that the publication of
the *Economic and Philosophical Manuscripts* was not only a defining
moment in the development of Marxism, but an event which played a
crucial role in the re-emergence of class struggle in the late 1960s:

> *The spirit of the young Marx animated the radical initiatives of the 1960s,*
> *from Berkeley to Prague; and even when political energy was crushed, as in*
> *the East, or when it dissipated itself, as in the West, this spirit survived.*[7]

The central idea of the *Economic and Philosophical Manuscripts* was
Marx's concept of alienation. In the essays Marx develops the idea that

capitalism turns activities which ought to give meaning to our lives—the work we do to transform our environment, the relationships we build with other people—into things that seem alien to us, outside of our control.[8] Ironically, capitalism which champions individual freedom stands between us and the 'free development of [our] physical and spiritual energies'.[9]

For the left wing intellectuals of the 1950s, cut off from the organised working class and living through the greatest boom in the history of capitalism, the concept of alienation was crucial to a defence of Marxism. As Berman argues, the *Economic and Philosophical Manuscripts* 'provided a searing indictment of capitalism even at its most triumphant.' It also laid the ground for the moral indictment of Stalinism, which Berman identifies with Marx's description of a 'crude, mindless communism'.[10]

The publication of the 1844 *Manuscripts* also recreated the sense of Marx's writings as 'work in progress' which had been hidden by decades of Stalinism. For Berman, even the unfinished form of Marx's work testifies to the flexibility and resilience of his thought.

> How can **Capital** end while capital lives on? To stop simply and abruptly, rather than create an ending, preserves far more of the truth that **Capital** has to tell: circling, spiralling, plunging one way and another, turning in upon himself, seeking endlessly for new axes to turn on, Marx kept his thought and his work as open-ended, and hence as resilient and long-lived, as the capitalist system itself.[11]

These trends are visible throughout *Adventures in Marxism*. For instance, Berman makes the point that Marx does not ever simply deal with the workings of impersonal social and economic forces. He never forgets that the contradictions of capitalism are worked out in real time, through real men and women.

There are two sets of voices in Berman's essays: firstly, the figures from the crowd scenes of history whom he brings to life—from the pages of *Capital*, among his students, or from the streets of New York. Secondly, there are the exceptional individuals whom he takes down from their pedestals, 'to confront [them] at ground level, the level on which we ourselves are trying to stand'.[12] Marx himself is of course the chief of these, but there are others, like the Hungarian Marxist Georg Lukács, the Soviet author Isaac Babel, and the German writer Walter Benjamin. In his essays these writers emerge as complex individuals, capable of reaching new heights of understanding, but also falling to great depths through personal anguish and suffering. Berman's Marx is an authentic bourgeois hero, grappling with new ideas in a lonely struggle to transcend suffering. In 'Marx: the Dancer and the Dance'

Berman describes 'the isolation and the anguish that were interfused with Marx's most radical creativity'.[13] He is 'one of the great tormented giants of the 19th century—alongside Beethoven, Goya, Tolstoy, Dostoevsky, Ibsen, Nietzche, Van Gogh—who drive us crazy as they drove themselves, but whose agony generated so much of the spiritual capital on which we all still live'.[14]

Likewise Lukács is 'one of the real tragic heroes of the 20th century', a man whose life was marked out with both personal and political tragedy—the suicide of his fiancee and the slow death of his Marxism in the stultifying atmosphere of Stalinist Russia. Yet after years of 'repudiating his thoughts and burying his feelings', Lukács finally redeems himself in rebellion against the Russian invasion of Hungary in 1956. On his deathbed:

[he] *condemns all communist regimes for betraying the original promise of communist revolutions: 'genuine socialist democracy...democracy of everyday life'... He sees capitalist and communist powers at home in a detente of domination, oppressing both their own and foreign people... 'Both great systems are in crisis. Authentic Marxism is the only solution'.*[15]

Berman's essay on Walter Benjamin is similarly shot through with intermingled personal and political tragedy. Benjamin hangs on to the last as the storm clouds gather across Europe, only fleeing as Hitler's armies close in on France. A friend persuades the US government to grant Benjamin a visa, but he is trapped in France, eventually committing suicide when his band of refugees is arrested on the border with Spain.

Adventures in Marxism is a collection of essays, written at different times for different audiences, rather than a polished work of theory or biography. However, the essays do encapsulate much of what excites Berman about Marx. Yet for all this, he also misses something vital. His heroic, epic Marx lacks any sense of organic connection to the only force which can turn his dreams of communism into reality: the working class. Berman's vision of the lonely thinker, struggling to lay bare the structures of capitalist society, is only one side of the picture. Marx did not simply demonstrate the role of the working class in overthrowing capitalism in the abstract—he spent a large part of his adult life testing out this idea through practical application. In his twenties Marx was active in the nascent Communist organisations of Europe. Despite the defeat of the revolutions of 1848 and his long periods of political inactivity, at the first signs of revival in the working class movement Marx threw himself back into the struggle with enthusiasm: organising, polemicising, writing pamphlets, speaking.

This aspect of Marx's life is not merely historical detail. Missing it out has profound implications for Marxist theory as a whole. Without this organic connection to the working class, Marxism has no living link to the forces within capitalist society which can ultimately overthrow it. It becomes a theory looking at society from the outside. This living connection allows Marxists to distil the experience of the most advanced sections of the working class, and to apply that experience to the theory itself. For instance, as John Molyneux argues, the specific form of the dictatorship of the proletariat 'was discovered neither by Marx nor any other Marxist theorist, but by revolutionary workers themselves' through the experience of the Paris Commune and the Russian Revolution[16]. Lenin, in his polemics with the Left Communists after the First World War, underlines the point:

Correct revolutionary theory...assumes final shape only in close connection with the practical activity of a truly mass and truly revolutionary movement.[17]

This is the missing heart of Berman's unfinished dialectic, the mechanism by which all the heat and light from the clash of titanic ideas turns into something concrete, something which is capable of overturning the social order.

Berman describes in the essay 'All that is Solid Melts Into Air' how for Marx the dynamism at the heart of capitalism pushes the system into unsustainable contradictions. Capitalism makes possible some of the greatest advances that humankind has ever known. Yet this is the same destructive system which wrecks and warps the lives of millions, which produces wars, crisis and famine in the midst of plenty. Berman argues that human beings do not just pay a material price for the contradictions within capitalism. For him, the bourgeoisie:

...is forced to close itself off from its richest possibilities, possibilities which can only be realised by those who break its power. For all the marvellous modes of activity the bourgeoisie has opened up, the only activity that really means anything to its members is making money.[18]

Berman sees the bourgeoisie cast in the role of the sorcerer's apprentice, who unleashes forces in the human personality which he cannot control: 'The more furiously bourgeois society agitates its members to grow or die, the more likely they will be to outgrow itself, the more furiously they will eventually turn on it as a drag on their growth'.[19] Berman's analysis here is revealing, as it again brings the contradictions of the system down to the level of the individual personality. The gap between what capitalism promises to individuals (personal freedom, choice and so on) and the restricted reality that most of us face does drive people to revolt. However, it is the system's failure to supply humanity's material needs that actually pushes the mass of workers to fight back. Marx always took the material conditions of capitalist society as the starting point for his arguments. As he famously stated, 'Men make their own history, but they do not make it just as they please; they do not make it under circumstances chosen by themselves'.[20] We do not choose the terrain we fight on, yet we fight in the knowledge that what we do shapes the struggle for future generations.

Reducing this struggle to subjective factors does not explain anything. Thus it is not simply the case, as Berman argues, that, 'by picturing themselves as unfree, men make themselves unfree: their prophecy of powerlessness is self fulfilling'.[21]

The contradictions within people's heads are reflections of contradictions in material reality. Workers under capitalism, because of their material position in society—their lack of control of the process of wealth creation—really are unfree. Their chains are not simply in their heads. Marx argued that it was vital for workers to recognise their subjection in order to overthrow it, but the working class cannot simply develop class consciousness and become free of the constraints of capitalism. There are echoes here of Edward Thompson's argument in his masterpiece, *The Making of the English Working Class*, where he effectively argues that class and class consciousness are the same thing.[22]

It is easy to understand how the idea of pure intellectual revolt against the system became attractive to the New Left, faced as it was with a dormant workers' movement dominated by Stalinism and triumphant capitalism. Perry Anderson argues that the whole tradition of Western Marxism was shaped by the defeat of revolution in Europe after the First World War:

> *...it developed within an ever-increasing scission between socialist theory and working class practice... To the exponents of the new Marxism that emerged in the West, the official Communist movement represented the sole embodiment of the international working class with meaning for them—whether they joined it, allied with it or rejected it.*[23]

The political tradition of this journal is based on the idea that what was wrong with Stalinist Marxism was that it was not Marxism at all, and that, likewise, what was wrong with Soviet Communism was that it was in fact a form of capitalism, state capitalism.[24] For the New Left, however, what was missing in Stalinist Marxism was a sense of humanity, or as Berman himself puts it, 'a sensual warmth and spiritual depth'.[25] Thus a large part of the New Left's criticism of the Communist parties depended on a moral rejection of Stalinism. Alaisdair MacIntyre, writing in the 1950s, argued that this stance led the rebels of the New Left 'to accept the role of isolated moral hero, who utters in the name of no one but himself'.[26] This could be an epitaph on Berman's vision of Marx—a tragic towering figure who rages against injustice and inhumanity but who ends up impotent and alone.

This isolation reflects the problems which the theoreticians of the New Left encountered when they tried to find a mechanism to resolve Marx's dialectic and break out of capitalist society altogether. Rejection of the Stalinist dominated workers' movements of the 1950s and 1960s often translated into rejection of the idea that workers can change society at all. For some of the key figures on the New Left this became the kind of pessimism personified by Herbert Marcuse. In his influential essays 'One Dimensional Man' and 'An Essay on Liberation' he argued that the modern working class had no longer any material interest in bringing down the system. Alaisdair MacIntyre argues that for Marcuse:

Human nature is infinitely malleable. The human nature of those who inhabit advanced industrial societies has been moulded so that their very wants, needs and aspirations have become conformist—except for a minority which includes Marcuse.[27]

There are echoes of this position in Berman's writing. For instance he argues, 'The workers may sustain each other today on the assembly line or on the picket line, only to find themselves scattered tomorrow among different collectivities, with different conditions, different processes and products, different needs and interests'.[28] Here Berman misses what is crucial about Marx's definition of class. What binds these workers together is not geographical location, nor the fact that they work for the same company, nor even that they do the same kind of job. For Marx, their position as workers is defined by their relationship to the means of production. This means that even if the factory closes and the former assembly line workers find themselves stacking shelves in a supermarket, they will remain workers, and retain fundamentally the same class interests and conditions.

Ironically, despite his celebration of change and dynamism in Marxism, Berman is left with a curiously static view of the working class. He misses the fundamental material forces which bind workers together, and which keep them in permanent antagonism to the bosses. He argues that Marx's claim that the working class is the force which can sweep away capitalism 'raises questions about [his] own romantic image of the working class. If being a paid wage labourer is the antithesis of having a halo, how can Marx speak of the proletariat as a class of new men, uniquely equipped to transcend the contradictions of modern life?'[29]

It is easy to look at the pressure of exploitation and oppression—and see the twisted wreckage it makes of all our lives—and despair of ever making the world anew. Building a communist society with the working class as it is, with all the baggage of reactionary ideas—racism, sexism, homophobia—and the contradictions that people carry around in their heads would be impossible. Socialists long before Marx recognised this problem. So their practical attempts to build a new society were based on a moral appeal to all classes to reject the horrors of capitalism. They tried to create an embryo of a co-operative, equal society by withdrawing from the world into communes, private utopias for the chosen few. Marx, however, starts from a different basis. As Alex Callinicos explains, 'The pressure of capitalist exploitation forces workers to organise and act collectively. Only thus can they tap the source of their real power, which springs from their position within capitalist relations of production...which gives [them] the power to abolish classes'.[30]

The working class does not stake its claim to restructure the future of humanity simply on grounds of moral superiority, but because its material position gives it the power to overthrow the entire social order. Marx's vision of the working class is not based on romanticism, but is grounded in reality. It is not a static vision of workers as they are, but one which contains the seeds of contradiction, change and struggle. Fighting side by side, workers begin to overcome the divisions which capitalist society forces onto them. They begin to realise the possibilities for change in a way which is almost impossible in everyday life. Workers occupying their factory in Chile during the revolution of 1972-1973 expressed the process like this: 'The bosses aren't going to tell us what to do... So we opened the stores, took out the raw materials, and just kept on producing—production didn't stop here for a single moment. And we won't stop now or ever. I think we've realised in these last few days that what we're defending is something more than just a plate of beans'.[31] Or as Marx put it, 'In the struggle...this mass [of workers] becomes united and constitutes itself as a class for itself. The interests it defends become class interests'.[32]

For all that he leaves out of Marx, Berman does a better job of capturing much of his spirit than many of his more orthodox defenders. John Rees's analysis of the New Left is also a useful comment on Berman's work: 'The New Left marked a renaissance in genuine Marxism, at last creating a tradition of analysis and debate beyond the sterility of Stalinism'.[33] Berman has kept alive his passion and enthusiasm for Marx for over 40 years. While many others on what he jokingly calls the 'Used Left' have given into academic despair, he has come through the hopes of the 1960s and defeats of the 1980s without losing the sense of exhilaration that he felt in the Four Continents bookstore. Like Marx, Berman never loses faith in the courage, determination and resilience of ordinary people, even when he cannot quite grasp how to turn those gut instincts into a force which can change society. His writing will inspire you, even when his conclusions are exasperating. Most of all he will make you want to go back to read and savour Marx, not as some literary curiosity, but as a living handbook for our confusing modern times:

> The 1990s began with the mass destruction of Marx effigies. It was the 'post-modern' age: we weren't supposed to need big ideas. As the 1990s end, we find ourselves in a dynamic global society ever more unified by downsizing, deskilling and dread—just like the old man said. All of a sudden, the iconic looks more convincing than the ironic; that classic bearded presence, the atheist as biblical prophet, is back just in time for the millennium. At the dawn of the 20th century, there were workers who were ready to die with *The Communist Manifesto*. At the dawn of the 21st, there may be even more who are ready to live with it.[34]

Notes

I would like to thank Dave Renton for his advice, for the loan of a large number of the books listed here, and in particular for drawing my attention to Alaisdair MacIntyre's article 'Notes from the Moral Wilderness'.

1   F Fukuyama, *The End of History and the Last Man* (London, 1992), p3.
2   K Marx, *Economic and Philisophical Manuscripts of 1844* (London, 1981).
3   M Berman, *Adventures in Marxism* (London, 1999), p8.
4   Ibid, p15.
5   J-P Sartre, *Iron in the Soul* (London, 1985), p311.
6   J Saville, 'Edward Thompson, the Communist Party and 1956', *Socialist Register* (London, 1994), p23. Quoted in J Rees, *The Algebra of Revolution* (London, 1998), p290.
7   M Berman, op cit, p21.
8   For a concise and well written explanation of Marx's concept of alienation, see J Cox, 'An Introduction to Marx's Theory of Alienation', *International Socialism* 79 (Summer 1998).
9   M Berman, op cit, p20.
10   Ibid, p20.
11   Ibid, p35.
12   Ibid, p255.
13   Ibid, p33.
14   Ibid, p33.
15   Ibid, p204.
16   J Molyneux, 'What is the Real Marxist Tradition?', *International Socialism* 20 (Summer 1983), p13.
17   V Lenin, 'Left Wing Communism: An Infantile Disorder', *Selected Works*, vol III (London, 1972), p378.
18   M Berman, op cit, p104.

19   Ibid, p108.
20   K Marx, *The 18th Brumaire of Louis Bonaparte* (Peking, 1978), p9.
21   M Berman, op cit, p45.
22   See J Rees, op cit, p294.
23   P Anderson, *Considerations on Western Marxism* (London, 1977), p92.
24   See T Cliff, *State Capitalism in Russia* (London, 1996), and *Trotskyism After Trotsky* (London, 1999).
25   M Berman, op cit, p21.
26   A MacIntyre, 'Notes from the Moral Wilderness', in K Knight (ed), *The MacIntyre Reader* (London, 1998), p34.
27   A MacIntyre, *Marcuse* (London, 1970), p88.
28   M Berman, op cit, p118.
29   Ibid, p137.
30   A Callinicos, *The Revolutionary Ideas of Karl Marx* (London, 1995), p142.
31   M Gonzalez, 'Chile 1972-73', in C Barker (ed), *Revolutionary Rehearsals* (London, 1987), p58.
32   K Marx, *Collected Works,* vol VI (London, 1976), pp210-211.
33   J Rees, op cit, p291.
34   M Berman, op cit, p266.

George Orwell: a literary Trotskyist?

A review of John Newsinger, **Orwell's Politics** *(Macmillan Press, 1999), £42.50*

ANNA CHEN

The millennium will mark the fiftieth anniversary of the death of George Orwell, critic, novelist, essayist and polemicist, and one of the best loved and most frequently quoted British authors of the century. The political consciousness pervading his writing makes him a touchstone for a wide range of readers and 'one of the major literary protagonists in the Cold War era'.[1] His last two novels, *Animal Farm* and *Nineteen Eighty Four*, are acknowledged as modern classics, while his experience of working class life in *Down and Out in London and Paris* and *The Road to Wigan Pier*, and of revolutionary struggle betrayed in *Homage To Catalonia*, continue to inform and inspire generations of socialists.

Orwell's writing was the source of as much controversy during his life as it was when left and right fought over his literary corpse after his death. The right claimed him for themselves, 'embracing him as an emotional conservative who had given terrible warning of the totalitarian logic inherent in the socialist cause',[2] while the Stalinist dominated left were willing to give away the man H G Wells once described as the 'Trotskyist with big feet'.[3] *Nineteen Eighty Four*, Orwell's final novel and a satire of Stalinist Russia, has been defined as 'the "canonical text" of conservative anti-Communism, as "the key imaginative manifesto of the Cold War" and gives Orwell the dubious honour of having "invented...a complete poetics of political invective".'[4] Isaac Deutscher, Marxist historian, famed anti-Stalinist and biographer of both Trotsky and Stalin, weighed into the debate, dismissing Orwell as 'a "simple minded anarchist" for whom any movement "forfeited its raison d'etre the moment it acquired a raison d'etat".[5] The 1970 publication of Orwell's miscellaneous writing under the title *The Collected Essays, Journalism and Letters* provided a context for Orwell's best known books and put the Stalinists and right wingers on the back foot as a new generation of socialists, unfettered by loyalty to the Communist Party, broke through the claims and counter-claims. And in 1980 Bernard Crick's exhaustively researched biography, *George Orwell: A Life*, lifted Orwell out of the quagmire of malice and misinformation and placed him firmly on the left, albeit as a *Tribune* socialist grown shy of revolutionary politics. However, even this mild reclamation of Orwell for the reformist left proved too much for adherents to the Communist tradition. Their reaction plumbed new depths with the publication in 1984 of *Inside The Myth: Orwell—Views from the Left*, a collection of essays attacking Orwell, edited by Christopher Norris and published by Lawrence and Wishart, a book which Newsinger calls 'an unholy alliance of feminists, cultural theorists and old fashioned Stalinists, dedicated to reversing his influence'.[6]

Orwell's Politics by John Newsinger moves the debate a critical step further. Taking the end of the Cold War as 'an ideal context for a reassessment' of Orwell's political ideas,[7] Newsinger gives us a map of Orwell's intellectual terrain, and deftly orientates the reader around the key Orwellian debates. He examines how Orwell's politics developed in a changing world, and extracts a throughline strung like a piano wire through volatile circumstances, warring ideologies and intellectual sleight of hand in the century that promised workers in the saddle. Newsinger's thesis is that, although Orwell's politics shifted throughout his lifetime, the one constant was his unwavering socialism. What detractors—and even some admirers—have missed is that he never ceased to write from within the left, attacking the betrayal of the revolution rather than the revolution itself.

Orwell gets a life

George Orwell was the name adopted by Eric Blair, the Eton educated son of a government official overseeing the opium trade. Born in India, Blair returned to the east to serve as an imperial policeman in Burma. He was by no means a socialist at this point. Conservative MP Christopher Hollis observed, following his visit to Burma in 1925, that Blair exhibited 'no trace of liberal opinions' and felt a particular loathing for Buddhist monks.[8] However, something was eating away at his conscience. In the opening chapter, entitled 'Pox Britannia', Newsinger charts Blair's changing attitude to the dirty job of maintaining order and breaking strikes. Prisons overflowed and villages were burnt to the ground. He returned to England in 1928 and later expressed his growing disgust with imperialism in fictional form in his first novel, *Burmese Days*, as well as in numerous articles and letters. His atonement was to put himself through the ordeals described in *Down and Out in London and Paris*, working as a dishwasher in a Paris hotel, and as a hop picker in Kent when he wasn't living as a tramp. In *The Road to Wigan Pier*, written in 1936, before he fought in Spain, and published in 1937, he stated his opposition to 'every form of man's dominion over man. I wanted to submerge myself, to get right down among the oppressed, to be one of them and on their side against the tyrants.' It is this determination to side with the oppressed that Newsinger sees setting Orwell on the road to socialism.[9]

Five years in Burma had transformed Eric Blair into 'George Orwell', a man who 'hated the imperialism I was serving with a bitterness which I probably cannot make clear'.[10] Step by step Newsinger shows us the developing line of Orwell's politics initially fuelled by that loathing. In one of his later 'As I Please' columns in *Tribune*,[11] Orwell was to connect the ruling classes' need for racism with their justification for imperialism. Satirising the British colonialists' absurd claims to racial superiority, he settled on the pith helmet as an 'emblem of imperialism' as it protected the supposedly thinner skull of the white master from the sun, whereas, we assume, Asiatic natives could happily fry while labouring like animals, their tiny brains protected by thick, simian, cranial bone.

Although Orwell acquired a small degree of fame with his first books, it was his experiences in Spain when he fought against Franco's fascists in the civil war, and the publication of his account of them in *Homage To Catalonia* and numerous articles, that put the revolutionary socialist cat among the Communist apparatchik pigeons. What he personally witnessed in Spain, above all else, turned Orwell against the Soviet Union and the international Communist movement, paradoxically driving him deeper into revolutionary socialism at the same time as he was being turned into a pariah among the left.

When Franco attempted the military coup on 17 and 18 July 1936, it had been held off only by a spontaneous uprising of the working class in many towns and cities. The Republican government remained paralysed. An armed working class took power in many Republican areas, and was particularly strong in Catalonia whose chief city was Barcelona. In his book *The Spanish Cockpit*, favourably reviewed by Orwell, Franz Borkenau describes revolutionary Barcelona. He notes the absence of any bourgeoisie or their agents, the police, who were replaced by armed workers' militias: 'Practically all the factory owners, we were told, had either fled or been killed, and their factories taken over by the workers'.[12] And all the churches had been burnt. It was so promising that Trotsky commented that in 'its political and cultural level, the Spanish proletariat stood on the first day of the revolution, not below, but above the Russian proletariat at the beginning of 1917'.[13] As Newsinger points out, 'Whether this revolution should be continued or reversed was to be the great political debate within the Republican camp, a debate finally settled by the Communists with police, torture chambers and execution squads'.[14]

The ensuing split among the anti-fascist forces broke down roughly along three lines. The first—Largo Caballero of the Socialist Party left wing, the socialist organisations, and the anarchists (FAI) and their trade union confederation, the CNT—took the initially dominant position that the revolution should be put on hold while Republican forces defeated the fascists. Caballero did not want the Republic overthrown by a workers' state but they agreed that once the military was crushed the revolution would continue. Adopting this attitude left the leaders of these organisations increasingly incapable of resisting the pressure they came under from the second group.

The second line was the deliberate slamming of the revolutionary process into reverse, liquidating all the revolutionary gains of July 1936, and re-establishing the bourgeois state. This was the policy adopted by the Republican middle class, but more surprisingly, this was also the line taken by the Spanish Communist Party, the Catalan Communists (PSUC) and supported by the Russian military-political machine. Communist policy in the 1930s was to unite left and centre parties as a Popular Front against right wing movements, which inevitably meant diluting the revolutionary content of their politics. Although the revolutionaries and the bourgeoisie were fighting *against* the same thing, ie fascism, they were fighting *for* mutually exclusive goals, ie capitalism and socialism. 'It is a combination,' wrote Orwell, 'with about as much vitality, and about as much right to exist, as a pig with two heads or some other Barnum and Bailey monstrosity'.[15] Orwell eventually realised, along with many others, that Russia was seeking a compromise with international capital in the form of an alliance with Britain and France. Russian foreign policy interests took precedence over supporting left wing movements in Europe: the revolution was marked for death.

Arguing against these positions were many individual anarchists and a small independent revolutionary party called the POUM, translated as the United Marxist Workers' Party, whose general secretary, Andreas Nin, was a former secretary to Trotsky. They believed that if the war was to be won the revolution had to be completed through the overthrow of the bourgeois state together with the continuation of the process of expropriation.

These, then, were the circumstances of Orwell's arrival in Catalonia to fight the fascists.

Orwell in Spain

Orwell's arrival in Barcelona, the reddest of Spanish cities, was, according to Crick, an accident.[16] Turned down for the International Brigade by the British Communist Party, Orwell eventually travelled to Spain under the auspices of the Independent Labour Party (ILP) in December 1936. Once in Barcelona, he signed up to the ILP affiliated POUM militia as 'Eric Blair: grocer'. He enthused over the tell tale signs of workers at least superficially in charge—or 'in the saddle'—finding them 'startling and overwhelming'. Newsinger describes it thus:

> *Buildings were draped with red flags or with the red and black flags of the anarchists, the walls were covered with the hammer and sickle and the initials of revolutionary organisations, and almost all the churches had been destroyed. The shops and cafes had been collectivised and the waiters and shop workers treated customers as equals. The trams and taxis were all painted black. Crowds of working class men and women filled the streets while loudspeakers played revolutionary songs. What particularly struck him was that as far as he could see the rich had disappeared. This was, he recognised, something worth fighting for. What Orwell had encountered in Barcelona was a working class that was becoming a class for itself.[17]*

The thrill wore off once he hit the front line. Orwell was dismayed by the conditions. As he says often in *Homage To Catalonia*, it wasn't so much the squalid state of the muddy trenches and drenched dugouts, or the terrifying abundance of rats, or the infestations of lice, or the human excrement caked everywhere that lowered his spirits—that was just war. It was the incessant boredom while waiting for action, the inadequate training, and the antiquated weaponry with which they were meant to fight the fascists stationed within eyesight that he found frustrating. His sympathies were by no means set when he arrived: he initially thought the Communists were right to concentrate on fighting Franco by building a more disciplined army. However, what kept him fighting for the POUM—even regretting later that he didn't join—was the realisation that the Communist line was effectively a counter-revolutionary one. It didn't merely stop the revolution in its tracks. It actually meant putting back the clock.

Orwell was deeply engaged in the debate around what to do about the revolution, siding with the most revolutionary line—to take the revolution forward. He thought it a mistake that the Republican government had been left in nominal control and was critical that, 'in spite of various changes in personnel, every subsequent government has been of approximately the same bourgeois-reformist character.' He explained that at first it didn't seem to matter, because the government was 'almost powerless'. The bourgeoisie were lying low, even disguising themselves as workers. But then, as power was grabbed by the 'Communists and right wing Socialists' and used in the interest of the Popular Front, 'the government was able to reassert itself, the bourgeoisie came out of hiding and the old division of society into rich and poor reappeared, not much modified'.[18] One by one the different parties composing the government were edged out by the Communists. Once Russia began to supply arms, a grateful Communist led Government came to heel and the success of the Spanish Communist Party was assured. Orwell explains how the Catalan Communists, the PSUC, were then able to recover power through 'a policy of pinpricks':

> *In every case, needless to say, it appeared that the thing demanded by military necessity was the surrender of something the workers had won for themselves in 1936... The process of [land] collectivisation was checked, the local committees were got rid of, the workers' patrols were abolished and the pre-war police forces, largely enforced and heavily armed, were restored, and various key industries which had been under the control of the trade unions were taken over by the Government...finally, most important of all, the workers' militias, based on the trade unions, were gradually broken up and redistributed among the new Popular Army, a 'non-political' army on semi-bourgeois lines, with a differentiated pay rate, a privileged officer caste, etc, etc.[19]*

He returned to Barcelona to find it just another bourgeois city, unrecognisable from the vibrant centre of workers' control he had seen only a few months earlier.

Trotsky had by now split with the POUM over their refusal to break away from the far greater numbers of anarchists and 'build their party as the revolutionary leadership of the Spanish working class... Instead, they hoped to persuade and influence the anarchists, who were the decisive force in Catalonia, into completing the revolution'.[20] Following a police attack on the CNT controlled telephone exchange in Barcelona on 3 May, working class Barcelona took to the barricades in defence of their rapidly eroding bastions of power. Unfortunately, both the POUM and CNT leaders vacillated instead of going on the offensive, giving the counter-revolutionary forces the upper hand. In a perverse twist of logic, the Communists accused Trotsky of leading the POUM alongside the fascists in a conspiracy against the Popular Front, his living several thousand miles away in Mexico and not being in touch with the Spanish comrades notwithstanding. The POUM was similarly slandered, firstly, as being 'objectively pro-fascist' because it was contradicting the Communist line to abandon the revolution, and then accused of actually fighting alongside the fascists, of sabotage and treason under Trotsky's orders. The official term for the POUM was 'Trotsky-Fascist', a libel that was repeated in newspapers across the world and used in support of the Moscow Show Trials. The *Daily Worker* called the ILP volunteers in Spain, many of whom were killed or wounded fighting fascism, a 'stain on the honour of the British working class'.[21] The propaganda war was vicious, the body count high and rising. Many were tortured by the dreaded secret police, languished in jail or were executed. Andreas Nin, a leading member of the POUM, was reportedly skinned alive. All were hounded by the Communists.

Orwell narrowly escaped but he had gained a whole new perspective. While convalescing from a fascist bullet in the throat, Orwell wrote to Cyril Connolly, telling him, 'I have seen wonderful things and at last really believe in Socialism, which I never did before'.[22] Although from his earlier publication *The Road to Wigan Pier* it was clear that he was at least intellectually committed to socialism, it was Spain that gave his socialism an emotional bedrock and dictated the course his socialism would take. Having witnessed the destruction of the revolution in Spain, and lost comrades in the Communist persecution of the POUM, that course would never lead to Moscow. In the preface to the Ukrainian edition of *Animal Farm* he wrote:

> *Nothing has contributed so much to the corruption of the original idea of Socialism as the belief that Russia is a Socialist country and that every act of its rulers must be excused, if not imitated. And so for the past ten years I have been convinced that the destruction of the Soviet myth was essential if we wanted a revival of the Socialist movement.*[23]

He returned to Britain to find that his association with POUM and his hostility to the Communists had left him alienated and marginalised in left circles. It was all but impossible to challenge the Communist version of events. His own publisher, Victor Gollancz, who controlled the Left Book Club with its massive readership, declined to publish *Homage To Catalonia* despite the success of *The Road to Wigan Pier* but Orwell refused to be gagged. His may have been a lone voice, but it was also a loud and clear one powered by a will to make itself heard through a torrent of articles and reviews.

Revolutionary patriotism and the Second World War

The Spanish Civil War was a pivotal point in Orwell's political development and the lessons learnt there coloured his politics for the rest of his life. The Hitler-Stalin Pact of August 1939—effectively carving Eastern Europe up between Germany and Russia—was another seismic world event that was to shake up his outlook and that of many Communists. Until that point Orwell had taken the ILP line of pacifism and internationalism but the pact reversed his position. He became staunchly pro-war, arguing in *Tribune*, the American literary journal *Partisan Review*, and his wartime broadcasts for the BBC that 'this war is a race between the consolidation of Hitler's empire and the growth of democratic consciousness'.[24]

Newsinger stresses the importance of the wartime *Searchlight* series of books, a platform for left writers to discuss 'war aims for a better future', co-edited by Orwell, and sees 'the whole series as a political intervention by Orwell at a time when he believed socialist revolution both imminently possible and urgently necessary'.[25] Orwell's own contribution, *The Lion and the Unicorn: Socialism and the English Genius*, the first of the series, propounded the view that patriotism was a material reality that overshadowed class hatred and internationalism. Orwell argued that the British working class had never acted internationally, citing the generally cool response to Franco's rise to power as an example, and so could not be relied upon to further the revolution alone. He dismissed the idea of an 'old fashioned' proletarian revolution in England and contended that any English socialist revolution would have to include the expanding middle class of professionals, higher paid skilled workers, media producers and technicians. These people, he insisted, were kept down by the ruling class and the system of private capitalism. 'Capitalism, he proclaimed, "simply does not work...cannot deliver the goods" and would have to be replaced by socialism if England was to defeat Hitler'.[26] Newsinger makes allowances for Orwell's patriotic excesses as a product of the times and as something he questioned towards the end of the war. For Newsinger, the core problem was that *The Lion and the Unicorn* was predicated on a faulty premise— that England in 1940-1941 was ripe for revolution. There were no signs of power moving into workers' hands even as late as 1942.

Orwell started to speak of a third way between the 'timid reformism' of the Labour Party and 'the 19th century doctrine of class war' of the Communists and Trotskyists. 'This third way, between reform and revolution, would, he believed, make it possible to carry through a socialist transformation of Britain that would nevertheless leave intact what he considered to be the essential qualities and character of the British national culture,' writes Newsinger, who adds:

> *It is this that makes Orwell such an uncomfortable political thinker: he was serious about both the desirability and necessity for socialism and about preserving national culture and character, propagating an almost mystical*

*patriotism. Most commentators have focused on his contribution to the elabo-
ration of the 'English Genius' ...and have neglected his call for a new socialist
movement that would reject both Communist-style revolution and Labour
Party reformism in favour of a third way to socialism, a third way that he continued to call revolutionary but that was adapted to modern conditions.*[27]

Commentators have suggested that Orwell moved away from revolution towards despair or reformist *Tribune* socialism some time towards
the end of 1942, but Newsinger shows him pursuing another route.
Certainly, faced with the reality that there would be no revolution in wartime Britain, Orwell reached an accommodation with British Labourism.
However, when assessing this period, Newsinger points out, what is
often overlooked is the absence of a British equivalent of the American
literary journal, *Partisan Review*, for which Orwell wrote the 'London
Letters' series of articles between 1941 and 1946. While the Communist
line may have dominated British left politics, it had no such clear run in
America. Originally committed to the viewpoint of 'the revolutionary
working class' and to 'defence of the Soviet Union',[28] the *Partisan
Review*, like Orwell, emerged from the fallout of 1936-1937 with a hostility to Stalinism and a broad sympathy for Trotsky's ideas. This
certainly qualifies Orwell as a 'literary Trotskyist', 'a creative writer and
commentator broadly influenced by Trotskyist ideas'.[29] Newsinger also
lists the catalogue of numerous Trotskyist pamphlets in Orwell's archive
to show that he had more than a passing acquaintance with Trotsky's politics: 'Clearly Orwell had a familiarity with Trotskyist politics that
academic commentators on his work have singularly lacked, with the
result that they have missed the extent to which much of his own political writing was a debate with the politics of the revolutionary left'.[30]

From 1941 Orwell fought for a 'revolutionary patriotic' line in the
anti-war *Partisan Review* against the 'revolutionary defeatist' editorial
line.[31] For Orwell and many others on the left the fate of the war was
inextricably bound up with the success of the revolution and the two
were inseparable. The crisis of the war came to a head in the early
summer of 1942 when it seemed possible that the left Labour politician
Stafford Cripps would provide significant leadership. By the end of the
summer the Conservatives had won power and the longed for growth in
popular consciousness failed to materialise. In January 1943 Orwell
wrote in *Partisan Review* that the 'crisis is over and the forces of reaction
have won hands down'.[32] He later apologised in his December 1944
'London Letter' for his 'many mistaken predictions', and went into a
lengthy self critical analysis of his 'very great error'. The war had been
won but the peace was lost. The survival of the ruling class had ended
any hope of socialism:

Britain is moving towards a planned economy, and class distinctions tend to dwindle, but there has been no real shift of power and no increase in genuine democracy. The same people still own all the property and usurp all the best jobs. [33]

What Newsinger crucially detects in this article is:

Orwell in the process of abandoning any serious hope of revolutionary change in the foreseeable future and coming to terms with the prospects of a Labour Government...as a 'lesser evil'. What he did not do, however, was repudiate his belief in the need for revolutionary change, for socialism, but merely acknowledged that he had been guilty of wishful thinking in believing it to be imminent. There was no lessening of his opposition to 'class distinctions and imperialist exploitation', no defection to 'the forces of reaction'. [34]

Skewering the Soviet myth

The accusation that he had abandoned socialism altogether intensified with the publication of *Animal Farm*. This allegorical fable, which Orwell wrote in response to Stalin's dissolution of the Comintern in 1943, earned him much enmity and a deliberate distortion of his very clear warning that Stalin was 'genuinely aiming at a closer tie up with the USA and Britain'.[35] The growing Russophile feeling in Britain since the Nazi invasion of Russia finished the Hitler-Stalin pact in June 1941 gave an added urgency to Orwell's objective. *Animal Farm* was finally published by Warburg in 1945 at the outset of the Cold War. Newsinger explains:

The fable offered little comfort to the conservative right. Not only did it wholeheartedly endorse the initial revolutionary act, it also went on implicitly to condemn the Soviet Union, not for being socialist, but for betraying socialism, for becoming indistinguishable in its conduct from the other great powers, for exploiting its own people and joining in the division of the world. [36]

Orwell's original intention was that *Animal Farm* should be an attack on the 1943 Tehran Conference and its aim that Stalin, Roosevelt and Churchill should carve the world up between them. When their alliance broke down the book was interpreted as an attack on revolution and socialism. Orwell later clarified his position, writing, 'I meant the moral to be that revolutions are only a radical improvement when the masses are alert and know how to chuck out their leaders as soon as the latter have done their job'.[37] Although Orwell placed responsibility for Stalin firmly with the Bolsheviks, even extending his criticism to Lenin and Trotsky, Newsinger is clear that he did not oppose revolution itself, having called for exactly that on numerous occasions over many years: 'All revolutions are failures,' he quotes Orwell's famous epigram, 'but they are not always the same failure'.[38]

His last novel, the disturbing dystopian vision of the future, *Nineteen Eighty Four*, written in 1948, was influenced by the Trotskyist critique of the Soviet Union. Originally written to attack both Fascist and Communist tyranny, the defeat of Nazism allowed Orwell to focus on the totalitarianism of the Russian state and the slavishness of the left intelligentsia that allowed the myth of Soviet 'socialism' to take hold. For Orwell it was the managerial class, of which the intelligentsia was one section, who would make the revolution alongside the working class, but who would also be repelled by the Soviet myth. He was appealing to them, warning what it would be like to be 'rigidly policed and controlled by an omnipotent terroristic apparatus that aspires to thought-control'.[39] He dissects the mentality of this 'middling' group and recounts Winston Smith's failed rebellion against Big Brother.

In Big Brother's world, the primary antagonist of the Party is 'Emmanuel Goldstein', once part of the Party's leadership, but subsequently expelled for a dizzying variety of crimes and betrayals. Goldstein is either the Party's greatest enemy, or else simply a bogeyman created by the Party as a focus for the society's fears, and as bait to lure potential rebels into showing their hands. The mysterious figure of Goldstein, object of the 'three minute hate' sessions, is a hybrid of Trotsky and the martyred Andreas Nin.[40] Goldstein's secret book at the heart of the story—entitled *The Theory and Practice of Oligarchical Collectivism*—was drawn from the Workers Party in America and their debates in the pages of *Partisan Review*, which argued that the Soviet Union was a bureaucratic collectivist society, rather than capitalist or socialist. Newsinger takes great pains to distance Orwell from James Burnham's *The Managerial Revolution* (which another Blair and his Third Way mentor seem to have swallowed wholesale), which claimed that the managerial class was the new ruling class, and locates, instead, *Nineteen Eighty Four*'s chief political influence in the writings of American Trotskyist Dwight Macdonald. For Macdonald, who debated fiercely with Burnham in *Partisan Review*, 'the bourgeoisie have been replaced by a new ruling class, the bureaucracy; capitalism has yielded to bureaucratic collectivism'.[41] In Russia and Germany, he insisted, supreme power lay with the political bureaucrats who directed the lowly managerial class to do their bidding. This is the world, recreated as Oceania with O'Brien as the personification of the ruling bureaucracy, inhabited by Winston Smith and his fellow managerial drones. Tony

Cliff later made a crucial contribution to this debate, advancing the theory of state capitalism—that the Russian bureaucratic ruling class needed to accumulate capital in order to compete with the superpowers rather than out of a simple lust for power.[42] The novel was also a fictional account of the nuclear stalemate Orwell dreaded, leading to 'the division of the world among two or three vast superstates, unable to conquer one another and unable to be overthrown by any internal rebellion'.[43] At the end of a pessimistic view of the future Winston Smith reaches the conclusion that hope for social transformation ultimately lies with the 'proles' when they realise their own massive potential. Winston the individual is broken, finally agreeing with Big Brother that two plus two does indeed make five.

Nineteen Eighty Four was immediately seized upon by the right to attack socialism which was equated with Stalinist Russia. In refusing to recognise that the Soviet Union was not socialist, the left found themselves wide open to these attacks. The most schizoid reaction must be Raymond Williams's dismissal of Orwell as an 'ex-socialist' in the same breath as he was apologising for Mao's Cultural Revolution, and Pol Pot and the Cambodian Khmer Rouge campaign: 'The revolutionary movement has to impose the harshest discipline on itself and over relatively innocent people in order not to be broken down and defeated'.[44] Orwell was never able to complete his defence of the book—that it was never intended as an attack on socialism or the British Labour Party—due to his illness from TB and his early death in 1950.

The fight over Orwell continues. He has been (mis)quoted by Thatcher, John Major, Rupert Murdoch and a bizarre raft of conservatives. Even recently centre-left columnist and Marx's biographer Francis Wheen invoked Orwell in *The Guardian* to justify the bombing of former Yugoslavia.[45] Comparing the tiny Balkan state of Serbia with Germany, which was the world's second most powerful industrial country at the outbreak of World War Two, and the petty nationalist dictator Slobodan Milosevic with Hitler, who represented the ideological last stand of capitalism in crisis, Wheen quotes Orwell on Hitler after the Hitler-Stalin pact and adds: 'Orwell would, I'd guess, be contemptuous of those who blame Nato for the horrific exodus from Kosovo.' Orwell believed in calling all sides of a conflict to account for their actions, and it would indeed be interesting to know if he would have had as much faith in the judgement and motives of the North Atlantic Treaty Organisation as Wheen. What we do know is that, on the subject of the left and war, Orwell had this to say:

Bullets hurt, corpses stink, men under fire are often so frightened that they wet their trousers... A louse is a louse and a bomb is a bomb, even though the *cause you are fighting for happens to be just... Our memories are short nowadays, but...dig out the files of **New Masses** or the **Daily Worker**, and just have a look at the romantic warmongering muck that our left wingers were spilling at the time. All the stale old phrases! And the unimaginative callousness of it! The sang-froid with which London faced the bombing of Madrid!... But here were the very people who for 20 years had hooted and jeered at the 'glory' of war, at atrocity stories, at patriotism, even at physical courage, coming out with stuff that with the alteration of a few names would have fitted into the **Daily Mail** of 1918. If there was one thing that the British intelligentsia were committed to, it was the debunking version of war, the theory that war is all corpses and latrines and never leads to any good result. Well, the same people who in 1933 sniggered pityingly if you said that in certain circumstances you would fight for your country, in 1937 were denouncing you as a Trotsky-Fascist if you suggested that the stories in **New Masses** about freshly wounded men clamouring to get back into the fighting might be exaggerated. And the Left intelligentsia made their swingover from 'War is hell' to 'War is glorious' not only with no sense of incongruity but almost without any intervening stage.*[46]

But then, as Bernard Crick has cautioned and Newsinger reminds us, all we can say with any degree of certainty is that if George Orwell was alive today, he'd be very old.[47]

Notes

1   J Newsinger, *Orwell's Politics* (Macmillan Press Ltd, 1999), pix.
2   Ibid, p155.
3   B Crick, *George Orwell: A Life* (Secker and Warburg, 1981), p294. To be precise, Orwell's feet were size 12. In Catalonia his boots had to be specially made.
4   J Newsinger, op cit, p122.
5   Ibid, p123, quoting Isaac Deutscher, '1984—the Mysticism of Cruelty', in Raymond Williams (ed), *George Orwell: a Collection of Critical Essays* (New Jersey, 1974), pp126-127.
6   Ibid, p156.
7   Ibid, pix.
8   Ibid, p4.
9   Ibid, p4.
10   G Orwell, *The Road to Wigan Pier*, quoted in J Newsinger, op cit, p3.
11   G Orwell, 'As I Please', *Tribune*, October 1944, in *The Collected Essays, Journalism and Letters*, vol 3 (Penguin, 1970), p299.
12   F Borkenau quoted in J Newsinger, op cit, p43.
13   L Trotsky, *The Spanish Revolution* (New York, 1973), p322, quoted ibid, p43.
14   Ibid, p43.
15   G Orwell, 'Spilling the Spanish Beans', *The Collected Essays, Journalism and Letters*, vol 1 (Penguin, 1970), p303.
16   B Crick, op cit, p208.
17   J Newsinger, op cit, p45.
18   G Orwell, 'Spilling the Spanish Beans', op cit, p304.
19   G Orwell, *Homage To Catalonia* (Penguin, 1989), p197.

20   J Newsinger, op cit, p163.
21   Ibid, p54.
22   G Orwell, *The Collected Essays, Journalism and Letters: Volume 1* (Penguin 1970), op cit, p269.
23   G Orwell, 'Author's Preface to the Ukrainian edition of *Animal Farm*', *The Collected Essays, Journalism and Letters*, vol 3 (Penguin 1970), p455. The Penguin edition notes, 'Orwell's original text has not been traced and the version given here is a recasting back into English from the Ukrainian translation.'
24   Ibid, p338.
25   J Newsinger, op cit, p72.
26   Ibid, p75.
27   Ibid, p77.
28   Ibid, p91.
29   Ibid, p91.
30   Ibid, p90.
31   Ibid, p93.
32   Ibid, p95.
33   G Orwell quoted ibid, p96.
34   Ibid, p96.
35   G Orwell quoted ibid, p98.
36   Ibid, p116.
37   G Orwell quoted ibid, p118.
38   Ibid, p118.
39   Ibid, p121.
40   B Crick, op cit, p246.
41   D Macdonald quoted in J Newsinger, op cit, p126.
42   For more on state capitalism, Newsinger recommends T Cliff, *Russia: a Marxist Analysis* (London, 1963), and C Harman, *Bureaucracy and Revolution in Eastern Europe* (London, 1974).
43   G Orwell quoted in J Newsinger, op cit, p152.
44   R Williams quoted ibid, p124.
45   F Wheen, 'Why We Are Right to Bomb the Serbs', *The Guardian*, G2 section, 7 April 1999, p4.
46   G Orwell, *The Collected Essays, Journalism and Letters*, vol 2 (Penguin 1970), 'Looking Back on the Spanish War' (Penguin, 1970), p288.
47   B Crick paraphrased in J Newsinger, op cit, pix.

History of theory

A review of Alex Callinicos, **Social Theory: A Historical Introduction**
(Polity, 1999), £14.99

ROB HOVEMAN

Alex Callinicos's latest book embodies all those qualities that have come to characterise his writing. *Social Theory* is elegantly and clearly written. It reflects an enormous range of reading and the assimilation of a wide range of often complex thinkers and theories. Anyone interested in social theory, especially undergraduate students working in the area of social studies, will find key theories succinctly encapsulated without loss of subtlety. They will also have their horizons expanded as Alex makes the compelling case for the inclusion of a much broader understanding of who should be counted as a social theorist than the more conventional hidebound bourgeois textbooks. For he does not just discuss the 'usual suspects' in terms of theorists of society—for example, Hegel, Marx, Durkheim and Weber—although there are excellent chapters devoted to each of them. He also discusses Darwin, Nietzsche, Freud, Lukács, Heidegger, Keynes and Hayek. And whilst this is obviously not the first book that someone new to Marxism would most benefit from, those who have a somewhat greater familiarity with the tradition will find the book very stimulating and edifying.

The social theories that emerged within the Enlightenment and since may be classified in three different ways according to their attitude to 'modernity', ie capitalism. The first approach is 'represented above all by Marx... He...kept his concept of history as a dialectical process motored by contradictions inherent in specific social formations. Civil society, or rather bourgeois society...is not the End of History, but simply a historically transitory social form whose claims to realise individual freedom are belied by its roots in capitalist exploitation. The Enlightenment aspiration to create an authentically rational society requires a further social revolution'.[1]

The second position is that of social theories which accept modern bourgeois society and provide a broad defence of it, modern liberalism being the prime example. Its theorists range from Tocqueville and Mill through Durkheim and Weber, who 'both make clear their emphatic belief that the hope of social revolution that will radically improve on actually existing modernity is the merest illusion', to Talcott Parsons. In examining these different thinkers Alex brings out some of the tensions in their attitude towards, and indeed reservations that some of them had about, modernity. Indeed, for summary descriptions of the principal views of these thinkers Alex's account can rarely have been bettered. He even makes Parsons, the dominant bourgeois sociologist in much of the post-war period (and someone I've always thought boring as well as politically reactionary), an interesting thinker whose views deserve comprehension and then rejection.

Finally there is the position taken by Nietzsche of radically rejecting modernity and the scientific rationality that the Enlightenment introduced. Nietzsche's philosophy was widely influential, particularly in Germany towards the end of the 19th and in the early decades of the 20th century. It had a key influence on Weber, even though Weber's social theory ultimately represents the acceptance of 'modernity' rather than its reactionary rejection. Later Nietzsche was to have a significant effect on one of the most influential and controversial philosophers and social theorists of the 20th century, Martin Heidegger, and then on the postmodernists, and particularly one of their most interesting theorists, Michel Foucault.

Social Theory takes a chronological approach, showing the development of the principal theories through the work of the most important theorists. Alex locates the development of these ideas in relation to economic, social and political developments of the day. However, there is no hint of reducing the ideas he deals with to some kind of passive reflection of the ideological needs of particular classes. Alex is well aware of the influence that preceding thinkers and theories have on serious social theorists, the manner in which they respond to pre-existing intellectual traditions and pursue their own intellectual curiosity and ability.

In one fascinating chapter he provides a brilliant summary of Darwin's theory of evolution, contrasting it with inaccurate pop versions of the theory that owe more to Lamarck. He then shows how Darwin's scientific theory is taken up and used in different ways by on the one hand the liberal, Spenser, and on the other by the Marxist, Kautsky. In the same chapter he goes on again to give a wonderfully concise summation of the principal elements of Nietzsche's theories with their extraordinary combination of 'naturalism which treats humankind as continuous with nature and an anti-naturalism which insists on what sets human beings apart from other species'.[2] Social Darwinism (eg Spenser's theories) and biological racism 'are repellent instances of naturalism; Weber is the most important champion of anti-naturalism; Marxism, even in its Kautskyan version, seeks to span the two traditions'.[3] Nietzsche's peculiarity lies in the way the 'human subject is naturalised, reduced to an incoherent cluster of biological drives, while nature is subjectivised, since all aspects of the physical as well as the social world are expressions of the will to power'.[4] In the space of just a few lines Alex once again deftly illuminates the similarities and differences between a wide range of diverse theories.

This is again brought out in Alex's treatment of Freud, a thinker profoundly influential on the 20th century mindset but not perhaps immediately obvious as a social theorist. Freud's significance, Alex argues, lies in 'the decisive step of cracking open the self and exposing the forces responsible for its constitution'.[5] Freud's theory of the mind is most important for establishing 'the most powerful and influential formulation of the concept of the unconscious'.[6] Again, for the single clearest, most concise and yet sufficiently comprehensive summary of Freud's principal theories over the space of just six pages, Alex cannot be surpassed.

It is here that I would like to enter a small reservation. Alex is, quite correctly, extremely impressed by the power and imagination of the intellectual edifice that Freud constructed. Nor can Freud's general influence on the spirit of the age be denied. Alex refers to the challenge Freud might appear to pose to the Enlightenment confidence in the use of reason, given the existence of hidden desires and drives, but seeks to show that Freud's work marked 'a major extension, and not the abandonment, of the Enlightenment project'.[7] He goes on to refer apparently favourably to attempts within the Frankfurt School, and in particular by Herbert Marcuse, to forge out of historical materialism and psychoanalysis a broader theory of human liberation. My reservation is that Freud's detailed theories seem unlikely to be true and some of the intellectual framework he brought to the study of the mind is lacking in coherence, and that there are therefore more profound criticisms that might be raised.

In another striking chapter Alex juxtaposes Lukács and Gramsci to Heidegger. Lukács and Gramsci represent a Hegelian reaction to the determinism of Second International Marxism, which had failed so abysmally in the face of the supreme test of the First World War. Lukács

and Gramsci in their different ways laid far greater emphasis on the subjective element in the historical process, the nature and development of
class consciousness compared to objective economic structures. Lukács
emphasised that 'reality can only be understood and penetrated as a
totality, and only a subject which is itself a totality is capable of this pen-
etration'.[8] It is only the working class which represents this subjective
totality and which therefore is the only class from whose standpoint
genuine understanding of capitalist society is possible, 'because the
transformation of labour power into a commodity is the real basis on
which that society is built'.[9]

Heidegger has been an immensely important figure, not so much in
this country with its more insular and parochial philosophical tradition,
but in continental Europe. He continues to exert a strong intellectual
influence in Germany, France and Italy. He is probably the single most
important intellectual influence on the doyen of the deconstructionist
postmodernists in France, Jacques Derrida. This is perhaps all the more
surprising since Heidegger warmly endorsed the coming to power of the
Nazi regime in 1933, endorsed or acquiesced in the purge of academics,
in particular Jews, upon his elevation at the Nazis' behest to Rector of
Freiburg University, and continued to support an idealised National
Socialism even when he became disappointed by actually existing
Nazism. Alex quotes the infamous letter he wrote to Marcuse in January
1948: 'I expected from "National Socialism" a spiritual renewal of life in
its entirety, a reconciliation of social antagonisms and a deliverance of
Western *Dasein* [human existence] from the dangers of communism'.[10]
He claimed soon to have recognised his 'political error', but, as Alex
points out, 'he nevertheless refused to condemn the extermination of the
Jews, comparing it to the expulsion of Germans from areas annexed by
Poland, Czechoslovakia and the Soviet Union at the end of the Second
World War'.[11]

Despite this despicable political background Heidegger was a serious
philosopher, particularly in his masterwork *Being and Time*, written in
the late 1920s before he was so politically compromised. Again Alex
provides a good summary of some of the principal ideas of what is a very
difficult work. A key intention of his analysis of *Dasein* is to overcome
the Cartesian dualism which had permeated much, but by no means all,
of Enlightenment thinking. Alex describes Heidegger's analysis of
'Being-in-the-world' as 'stunning', 'one of the great philosophical
achievements of the 20th century'.[12] I confess to being somewhat less
stunned by Heidegger's analysis, and I do not believe that Heidegger
successfully overcomes some of the persisting philosophical problems
concerning the relationship of human beings to a reality beyond them
and to other human beings themselves. Be that as it may, Heidegger is

interestingly portrayed as a thinker who is responding to the tumultuous times of the 1920s, a social world 'as alienated as that evoked by Lukács in his theory of reification. But, unlike Lukács, he finds no agency internal to this world that offers an escape'.[13] Alex quotes Richard Wolin's observation that, for Heidegger, 'once the inauthenticity of all traditional social norms has been existentially unmasked, the only remaining basis for moral orientation is...a radical assertion of will...unconstrained by the impediments of social convention'.[14] And here we can discern the link, albeit underdetermined, between Heidegger and Nietzsche, and Heidegger and Hitler, even though his relationship to both came some years later.

Many readers will be most eager to reach the sections of the book which deal with more contemporary thinkers and arguments. Alex demonstrates, however, that an understanding of the intellectual history and tradition of social theorising can be crucial to getting a handle on more contemporary thinkers and their strengths and vulnerabilities. In the last two chapters of the book Alex comes into the more contemporary period, examining the structuralism of Levi-Strauss and Althusser, the post-structuralism of Foucault, and the theories of Habermas and Bourdieu, the latter a leftist French intellectual who has actively supported the oppositional movements which started with the wave of public sector strikes in France in 1995. He goes on to examine the views of Ulrich Beck and Anthony Giddens.

Alex identifies the limitations of the Saussurean model of language on which the structuralists drew so heavily, and his brief portrayal of Althusser's theories seems unsympathetic to Althusser's project in just about every respect. In particular Alex contrasts Althusser's claim that 'history is a process without a subject', with the theories of Gramsci and Lukács.[15] The intellectual weaknesses of structuralism made it an easy target for the disillusioned post-1968 post-structuralists. As Alex puts it, the 'conceptual flaws of Althusserian Marxism thus meant it was liable to collapse into something much closer to the kind of Nietzschean social theory which began to gain ground in the mid-1970s'.[16] The key figure in this process was Michel Foucault. Ironically, for all the talk of the rejection of 'grand narratives', Foucault's underlying theory was just as much a grand narrative, if a less sophisticated one, than Marx's attempts to provide a theory of the capitalist system. And for all the brilliance of some of Foucault's detailed historical and social analyses, his underlying philosophy ultimately lacked coherence. The all-pervasiveness of the 'will to power' denied him a vantage point from which he could legitimately claim to have got to the truth about the systems of domination he sought to analyse, and provided no coherent ground on which to theorise resistance to that domination. Alex's comprehensive demolition of the whole postmodernist edifice in *Against Postmodernism* is briefly but very usefully echoed in the critique of Foucault.

Alex's views on Habermas, Giddens and Bourdieu have been expounded at some length in other publications. He is more in favour of Habermas and Bourdieu, who have retained a critical edge to their work, and less in favour of Beck and Giddens, as one might expect, although he detects vulnerabilities and weaknesses in all four. In the final chapter he gives reasons to reject the novelty and validity of the critique of modernity offered by Foucault, Deleuze and Derrida in particular. He also points out the ambiguity of the term 'modernity' as it has been used by social theorists. There is the philosophical idea of modernity as 'the historical realisation of the Enlightenment's conception of a present which justifies itself by its difference from the past it leaves behind and by the indefinite progress it will achieve in the future'.[17] Secondly, there is the view that modernity refers to a particular kind of society, and thirdly, that it is a particular form of experience within society. Alex gently teases out the differences in these conceptions in order then to test out the theories, particularly those of Giddens and Beck, which have come to dominate the academy and which prefer to deploy the concept of modernity to that of capitalism.

Alex claims that 'most versions of social theory would benefit from a dialogue with a naturalistic conception of the world which recognises the continuities between both the physical and social worlds and the forms of understanding appropriate to them, but which does not suppress or ignore the discontinuities between them'.[18] On this Alex is undoubtedly right. He has never been afraid to draw on and develop theory where he feels there are legitimate questions which even the best of the classical Marxist tradition has either not addressed or not answered adequately. *Social Theory* shows the same commitment to understand our enemies' theories, the better to contest them intellectually and shore up any weaknesses on our side.

Alex goes on to argue that the widespread tendency amongst contemporary social theorists towards a pessimism about the possibility of radical social change is not just the product of a reasonable induction from the historical experience of the 20th century, but has material roots in the increasingly narrow specialisms of academic life, cut off from political activity and practice. Even Bourdieu's call for an 'International of intellectuals committed to defending the autonomy of the universes of cultural production',[19] whilst progress itself 'serves to underline how deeply entrenched the idea of a radical disjunction between theory and practice has become among those intellectuals who seek to situate it historically and sociologically'.[20]

Alex finishes by arguing that the attempt to silence Marx will not be so easily accomplished. Marx's analysis of capitalism remains unsurpassed. Firstly, he saw capitalism as a dynamic mode of production spreading out and coming to dominate the whole of the world, an extraordinarily prescient analysis which has finally come to pass at the end of the 20th century. Secondly, Marx saw that the dynamism was beset by chronic instability, an instability which destroys production and lives and which exposes as nonsense the claim that capitalism is the 'fairest and most rational way of meeting humankind's economic needs'.[21] Thirdly, 'there is a necessary connection between the process of capital accumulation and the exploitation of wage-labour. In remaking the world, capitalism creates a class of workers who over time will develop the numbers, cohesion and self-organisation necessary to revolutionise society'.[22] 'Social theory...belongs to the heritage of the Enlightenment...spurred on by the voice of the radicalised Enlightenment, social theory can become what the philosophers believed reason to be, a force for liberation'.[23] Alex's excellent and timely book is a significant contribution to increasing the chances of social theory becoming that force for liberation.

Notes

1 A Callinicos, *Social Theory* (Cambridge, 1999), p56.
2 Ibid, p115.
3 Ibid, p115.
4 Ibid, p115.
5 Ibid, pp188-189.
6 Ibid, p189.
7 Ibid, p193.
8 Quote from Lukács, ibid, p207.
9 Ibid, p207.
10 M Heidegger, Letter to Herbert Marcuse, 20 January 1948, reprinted in R Wolin (ed), *The Heidegger Controversy* (Cambridge, Massachusetts, 1993), p162.
11 A Callinicos, op cit, p217.
12 Ibid, p219.
13 Ibid, p220.
14 R Wolin, *The Politics of Being* (New York, 1990), p39, quoted in A Callinicos, op cit, p221.
15 L Althusser, *Politics and History* (London, 1972), p183, quoted in A Callinicos, op cit, p270.
16 Ibid, p276.
17 Ibid, p297.
18 Ibid, p306.
19 P Bourdieu, *The Rules of Art* (Cambridge, 1996), p344, quoted in A Callinicos, op cit, p310.
20 Ibid, p310.
21 Ibid, p316.
22 Ibid, p316.
23 Ibid, p318.

Comment on Molyneux on art

CHRIS HARMAN

John Molyneux has ferociously defended his definition of art as 'unalienated labour' (*International Socialism* 84) in his reply to the mild comments made by Chris Nineham (*International Socialism* 82). But Chris cannot be the only one to question John's definition.

I find it unsatisfactory for one simple reason. It does not provide us with any criterion for distinguishing good art from bad art. Say someone enjoys playing the piano (or even singing in the shower) and does so out of tune. What they are engaged in certainly is not the direct production of commodities, and it is certainly not alienated labour according to the brief definition given by John from Marx's 1844 writings. We might even want to call it 'art'—but we would usually go on to insist it is bad art. The same applies to thousands of novels and poems (published as well as unpublished), and even to some paintings which make it into exhibitions and fetch high prices.

John himself implies a distinction between 'good art' and 'bad art' when he makes (probably justified) derogatory comments about one of the most famed artists of the 20th century, Salvador Dali, and criticises some of the contributions to the 'Sensation' exhibition (especially the Chapmans'). But his own definition of art provides no basis for trying to distinguish the good from the bad. Providing it is done in an unalienated way, pushpen is, it seems, as good as Pushkin.

At one point John seems to recognise the need for a more refined definition. He moves away from saying that art is simply unalienated labour to asserting that in art 'the form is the content'. But in itself this characterisation, close to the old one of 'art for the sake of art', does not take us any further forward. It does not provide any criteria for judging the form other than by pure subjective preference—ie 'it is good because I like it.' Yet John himself relies, in practice, on such criteria. His review of the 'Sensation' exhibition said some things about the works of Damien Hirst which were interesting, whether you fully agree with them or not. They were not, however, restricted to a mere discussion of form. They, quite rightly, included references to what he thought the form was trying to express.

In fact, the whole issue of alienated and unalienated labour is a diversion. There have been societies in which all labour was unalienated and in which visual representation, music, storytelling and poetry were part of everyday life. Such, for instance, seems to have been the case with the Mbuti 'pygmies' of the Congo rainforests, as described in Colin Turnbull's *The Forest People*. In a society without classes, labour, even unpleasant labour, rises straight out of people's immediate needs and does not take on a life of its own, over and against them. This, however, ceases to be the case once classes have arisen. Property relations, state structures and ideological institutions which once arose out of the needs of production now weigh down on people as an external force—in the process inhibiting further advances of production. It is at this point that 'art' begins to emerge as a form of activity compartmentalised off from the rest of life. It is part of the overall process of the development of alienation.

John reduces the question of alienated labour simply to the question of commodity production. When you produce for the market, according to John, you are involved in alienated labour; when you produce for yourself you are not. He measures Chris's comments about alienation and art up against this definition, using a single quotation from Marx as his benchmark, rather in the manner of a multiple-answer test paper, and finds Chris amiss. Using the same benchmark, he finds as unalienated do-it-yourself activity (which I will remember the next time I have to cut the lawn or paint the bathroom), and even the toil which the serf family is compelled to undertake to feed itself after providing forced labour in the fields of the feudal lord. According to John's argument, housework cannot be alienated labour either.

This is pure logic-chopping. Marx's notion of alienation is not contained in one or two sentences, but rather describes the whole process by which humans are dominated by their past production. The process reaches its highest form under capitalism, but occurs in all class societies. That is why Marx could accept (while deepening) Feurbach's understanding of religion as a form of human alienation.

Capitalist society in its totality is organised around the production and circulation of the alienated labour of human beings. This dominates their whole life activity. They are engaged in an alienated activity when they labour to reproduce their own labour power so that someone else can exploit it (ie when workers are involved in housework or do-it-yourself, or when peasants labour on their own plots). They are also alienated when, in trying to do other things for enjoyment or self expression, they are continually forced to worry about coping with the realities of class society. Marx and Engels certainly did not restrict the notion of alienation simply in the narrow economistic way attempted by John. Take, for instance, Marx's comment on money in the 1844 manuscripts: 'The power to confuse and invert all human and natural qualities, to bring about the fraternisation of incompatible, the divine power of money resides in its essence as the alienated and exteriorised species-life of men. It is the alienated power of humanity.'

In *The Holy Family* Marx and Engels even apply the notion of alienation to the ruling class: 'The possessing class and the proletarian class express the same human alienation. But the former is satisfied with its situation, feels itself well established in it, recognises this alienation as *its own power*, and thus has the appearance of *human existence*.' If the exploited class and the exploiting class are both alienated, it is difficult to see how artists can magically avoid the condition—especially when they have to sell the products of their artistic labours in order to live. We live in a world of alienation, from which there is no simple escape back to the unalienated forms of aesthetic expression to be found under primitive communism.

John twice uses the same quote from Marx about Milton in order to try and back up his case (in both his original article and in his reply to Chris): 'Milton produced *Paradise Lost* for the same reason that silkworms produce silk. It was an activity of his nature.'

According to John, this passage describes *Paradise Lost* as the product of unalienated labour, and therefore, he concludes, art can be defined as unalienated labour. There is, of course, an elementary logical mistake in the argument (a false syllogism of the form, 'Swans are a product of the act of mating, and therefore birds can be defined as things produced by the act of mating'). But more importantly, John has not given any thought to whether Marx's comment could possibly be true if taken literally. Did Milton really write *Paradise Lost* through a simple, natural process akin to that of the worm exuding silk threads? I'm not a great expert on either Milton or *Paradise Lost*, but I understand the poem was a product of Milton's anguish in the forlorn years after the defeat of the English Revolution in 1660. He had set out, he wrote, 'to justify the ways of God to Man'. In other words, he was grappling, through using a poetic form, with the realm of alienation. Of course, he was not producing poems on a production line for a paymaster. But he was still labouring within a whole world of alienation. The success or failure of his project could not be measured in terms of a definition of art as 'unalienated' labour, nor in terms of the 'form being the content'. The form had to give expression to the content in a special way, but certainly could not be identified with it.

In fact, all artists suffer from a profound version of alienation. Art, like language, cannot exist for the individual alone. The individual painter, musician, filmmaker or whatnot is attempting to communicate something to other people. But the means by which artists can communicate are not in their own hands in a class society. They belong to those who own the other means of production, the members of the ruling class. Even when artists do not have to sell their labour power in order to live, they have to sell its products in order to be able to communicate. In a capitalist society their very ability to function depends upon their ability to get access to the market, just as in pre-capitalist societies it depended on their finding patrons. The entrepreneur or patron stands between the artist and the audience. Alienation is an inescapable feature of the artistic condition. The only question is the degree to which the artist makes the compromises necessary to be happy in his or her alienation.

The connection between alienation and art is very different in kind to that claimed by John. But even when properly grasped, the connection alone does not explain why some art is good, or even 'great', and much lousy. After all, there have been good artists who have seemed happy with bourgeois society and many bad artists who have hated it. We judge whether they are good or bad not on the basis of their personal feelings of alienation, but on the basis of something else entirely.

Amazingly, John does not even consider what this can be, except in his reference to the form being the content. Yet only at its simplest level is excellence in art about pure form (beautiful shapes, words or sounds, or entertaining stories). To restrict ourselves to that level would be a nursery rhyme, doggerel or muzak approach to art. Any art above this minimal level involves an attempt at communication. It is an attempt by one person to convey feelings, emotions or a view of the world to others. That is why much very good art hurts as well as pleases, produces feelings of anguish as well as those of joy, and can be unpleasant as well as pleasant (in the way John himself claims is true of Damien Hirst's sharks). It is precisely this reaching out beyond the simply aesthetic or pleasurable that makes Beethoven's symphonies, Verdi's arias or Billy Holliday's songs superior examples of art.

Art in this sense is representational. By this I don't mean it has to be a picture of reality. But it has to convey something about reality to other people. It does so by techniques very different to that of the simple box camera or recording machine (although in the right hands these too can produce art). It does not attempt to be a carbon copy of reality. Nevertheless, it has real references. What are these?

Volosinov writes in his essay 'Discourse in Life and Discourse in Art' (translated as an appendix to his *Freudianism, A Critical Sketch*):

*Formalist aesthetics...defines artistic forms as **the form of the material**. If this point of view is to be carried out consistently, content must necessarily be ignored... So understood form loses its active, evaluative character and becomes a mere stimulus of passive feelings of pleasure in the perceiver...*

But, he continues:

The importance of form has to do not with the material, but with the content...Through the agency of artistic form the creator takes up an active position with respect to content. The form in and of itself need not necessarily be pleasurable; what it must be is a convincing evaluation of the content.

Voronsky, in his essay 'Art as the Cognition of Life' (translated in 1998 in the book of the same title), writes:

*Art is not the free play of fantasy, feelings or moods; art is not the expression merely of the subjective sentences and experiences of the poet; art is not assigned the goal primarily of awakening in the reader 'good feelings'. Like science, art cognises life. Both art and science have the same subject: life, reality. But science analyses, art synthesises; science turns to the mind of man, art to his sensual nature. Science cognises life with the help of concepts, art with the aid of images in the form of living, sensual contemplation... The genuine poet, the genuine artist, is one who **sees** ideas... Like science, art gives **objective truths**; genuine art demands precision because it deals with the object, it is empirical.*

None of this means that art is a simply reproduction of reality. 'Life' embraces the whole gamut of human experiences, emotions and feelings in relation to the natural and social worlds. Deepening human knowledge of these things involves deepening human sensibilities to them, in a way that is not simply reducible to the abstract understanding provided by science (and the historical science of Marxism).

The different arts use different methods. They employ, so to speak, different languages. A work of art can only be understood through the particular language of its field. You cannot judge a Beethoven symphony in the same way you judge a Stendhal novel (even if they contain some similar themes). But that does not mean that the language, the form, stands alone, independent of its content, or that somehow it is the content. Art is not simply unalienated labour, 'art for the sake of art' (*ars gratia artis*, as MGM used to insist in Latin on its logo). Or, at least, what most of us think of as good art is the product of attempts by artists to come to terms with life around them. In the modern world, that means grappling with alienated life within capitalist society (together with the new forms of life trying to break out of it). That is why there is unresolved tension in any such art, whether painting, film, the novel, poetry or music.

The difference between a great piece of classical music or jazz and a trite pop song is not that one provides an explicit political stance and one does not. It is that one extends our own sensitivity to the range of human feelings, whether of torment, exhilaration or simply contendedness, in a world torn apart by contradiction. By contrast, the other anaesthetises our sensibilities. To that extent, one is true to the world around us, the other false. One helps us challenge that world, even if the artist who produces it is personally conservative. The other helps us, rather as a heavy swig of alcohol might, to tolerate that world, even if the artist is personally very left wing.

In writing about the 'Sensation' exhibition John Molyneux gave implicit recognition to some this. He employed criteria other than 'unalienated labour' or 'the form in the content' to provide critical insights. That is why I for one found his piece illuminating (although, unfortunately, it came out too late for me to get the chance to go to the exhibition and judge the different works of art myself). But in his article defending modern art and in his attack on Chris Nineham he rules out precisely such criteria.

A last couple of points. I think John has been diverted up the barren 'unalienated labour' path because of his original starting point—his belief that there is some great argument about the validity of something called 'modern art'. I have not come across this as a serious argument outside the tabloid press for about 30 years at least. The arguments I come across are about certain, present-day artists, which is a different matter entirely. For some reason, he seems to think that anyone who differs with his judgements on other *artists* is joining a backward looking rejection of most of the art that appeared in the 20th century. Hence a definition which seems to endorse virtually anything as art.

There are real arguments to be taken up about the way different forms of art have developed as capitalism has engulfed the world. Trotsky, Lukács, Brecht, Volosinov and Voronsky have all approached such arguments from different angles, so as to evaluate different artists, trends and schools. John's piece on the 'Sensation' exhibition was a useful endeavour to go in the same direction. Unfortunately, such efforts are not helped by his formulation of a mistaken definition of what art is.

The Socialist Workers Party is one of an international grouping of socialist organisations:

AUSTRALIA	International Socialists, PO Box A338, Sydney South
BRITAIN	Socialist Workers Party, PO Box 82, London E3
CANADA	International Socialists, PO Box 339, Station E, Toronto, Ontario M6H 4E3
CYPRUS	Ergatiki Demokratia, PO Box 7280, Nicosia
DENMARK	Internationale Socialister, PO Box 5113, 8100 Aarhus C
GERMANY	Linksruck, Postfach 304 183, 20359 Hamburg
GREECE	Sosialistiko Ergatiko Komma, c/o Workers Solidarity, PO Box 8161, Athens 100 10
HOLLAND	Internationale Socialisten, PO Box 92052, 1090AA Amsterdam
IRELAND	Socialist Workers Party, PO Box 1648, Dublin 8
NEW ZEALAND	Socialist Workers Organization, PO Box 8851, Auckland
NORWAY	Internasjonale Socialisterr, Postboks 9226 Grønland, 0134 Oslo
POLAND	Solidarność Socjalistyczna, PO Box 12, 01-900 Warszawa 118
SPAIN	Socialismo Internacional, Apartado 563, 08080 Barcelona
UNITED STATES	International Socialist Organisation, PO Box 16085, Chicago, Illinois 60616
ZIMBABWE	International Socialist Organisation, PO Box 6758, Harare

The following issues of *International Socialism* (second series) are available price £3 (including postage) from IS Journal, PO Box 82, London E3 3LH. *International Socialism* 2:58 and 2:65 are available on cassette from the Royal National Institute for the Blind (Peterborough Library Unit). Phone 01733 370777.

International Socialism 2:84 Autumn 1999
Neil Davidson: The trouble with 'ethnicity' ★ Jim Wolfreys: Class struggles in France ★ Phil Marfleet: Nationalism and internationalism ★ Tom Behan: The return of Italian Communism ★ Andy Durgan: Freedom fighters or Comintern army? The International Brigades in Spain ★ John Molyneux: Art, alienation and capitalism: a reply to Chris Nineham ★ Judy Cox: Dreams of equality: the levelling poor of the English Revolution

International Socialism 2:83 Summer 1999
John Rees: The socialist revolution and the democratic revolution ★ Mike Haynes: Theses on the Balkan War ★ Angus Calder: Into slavery: the rise of imperialism ★ Jim Wolfreys: The physiology of barbarism ★ John Newsinger: Scenes from the class war: Ken Loach and socialist cinema ★

International Socialism 2:82 Spring 1999
Lindsey German: The Blair project cracks ★ Dan Atkinson and Larry Elliott: Reflating Keynes: a different view of the crisis ★ Peter Morgan: The new Keynesians: staking a hold in the system? ★ Rob Hoveman: Brenner and crisis: a critique ★ Chris Nineham: Art and alienation: a reply to John Molyneux ★ Paul McGarr: Fascists brought to book ★ Brian Manning: Revisionism revised ★ Neil Davidson: In perspective: Tom Nairn ★

International Socialism 2:81 Winter 1998
Alex Callinicos: World capitalism at the abyss ★ Mike Haynes and Pete Glatter: The Russian catastrophe ★ Phil Marfleet: Globalisation and the Third World ★ Lindsey German: In a class of its own ★ Judy Cox: John Reed: reporting on the revolution ★ Kevin Ovenden: The resistible rise of Adolf Hitler ★

International Socialism 2:80 Autumn 1998
Clare Fermont: Indonesia: the inferno of revolution ★ Workers' representatives and socialists: Three interviews from Indonesia ★ Chris Bambery: Report from Indonesia ★ Tony Cliff: Revolution and counter-revolution: lessons for Indonesia ★ John Molyneux: The legitimacy of modern art ★ Gary McFarlane: A respectable trade? Slavery and the rise of capitalism ★ Paul McGarr: The French Revolution: Marxism versus capitalism ★ Shaun Doherty: Will the real James Connolly please stand up? ★

International Socialism 2:79 Summer 1998
John Rees: The return of Marx? ★ Lindsey German: Reflections on *The Communist Manifesto* ★ Judy Cox: An introduction to Marx's theory of alienation ★ Judith Orr: Making a comeback: the Marxist theory of crisis ★ Megan Trudell: New Labour, old conflicts: the story so far ★ John Molyneux: State of the art ★ Anna Chen: In perspective: Sergei Eisenstein ★ Jonathan Neale: Vietnam veterans ★ Phil Gasper: Bookwatch: Marxism and science ★

International Socialism 2:78 Spring 1998
Colin Sparks: The eye of the storm ★ Shin Gyoung-hee: The crisis and the workers' movement in South Korea ★ Rob Hoveman: Financial crises and the real economy ★ Peter Morgan: Class divisions in the gay community ★ Alex Callinicos: The secret of the dialectic ★ John Parrington: It's life, Jim, but not as we know it ★ Judy Cox: Robin Hood: earl, outlaw or rebel? ★ Ian Birchall: The vice-like hold of nationalism? A comment on Megan Trudell's 'Prelude to revolution' ★ William Keach: In perspective: Alexander Cockburn and Christopher Hitchens ★

International Socialism 2:76 Autumn 1997
Mike Haynes: Was there a parliamentary alternative in 1917? ★ Megan Trudell: Prelude to revolution: class consciousness and the First World War ★ Judy Cox: A light in the darkness ★ Pete Glatter: Victor Serge: writing for the future ★ Gill Hubbard: A guide to action ★ Chris Bambery: Review article: Labour's history of hope and despair ★

International Socialism 2:75 Summer 1997
John Rees: The class struggle under New Labour ★ Alex Callinicos: Europe: the mounting crisis ★ Lance Selfa: Mexico after the Zapatista uprising ★ William Keach: Rise like lions? Shelley and the revolutionary left ★ Judy Cox: What state are we really in? ★ John Parrington: In perspective: Valentin Voloshinov ★

International Socialism 2:74 Spring 1997
Colin Sparks: Tories, Labour and the crisis in education ★ Colin Wilson: The politics of information technology ★ Mike Gonzalez: No more heroes: Nicaragua 1996 ★ Christopher Hill: Tulmults and commotions: turning the world upside down ★ Peter Morgan: Capitalism without frontiers? ★ Alex Callinicos: Minds, machines and evolution ★ Anthony Arnove: In perspective: Noam Chomsky★

International Socialism 2:73 Winter 1996
Chris Harman: Globalisation: a critique of a new orthodoxy ★ Chris Bambery: Marxism and sport ★ John Parrington: Computers and consciousness: a reply to Alex Callinicos ★ Joe Faith: Dennett, materialism and empiricism ★ Megan Trudell: Who made the American Revolution? ★ Mark O'Brien: The class conflicts which shaped British history ★ John Newsinger: From class war to Cold War ★ Alex Callinicos: The state in debate ★ Charlie Kimber: Review article: coming to terms with barbarism in Rwanda in Burundi★

International Socialism 2:72 Autumn 1996
Alex Callinicos: Betrayal and discontent: Labour under Blair ★ Sue Cockerill and Colin Sparks: Japan in crisis ★ Richard Levins: When science fails us ★ Ian Birchall: The Babeuf bicentenary: conspiracy or revolutionary party? ★ Brian Manning: A voice for the poor ★ Paul O'Flinn: From the kingdom of necessity to the kingdom of freedom: Morris's *News from Nowhere* ★ Clare Fermont: Bookwatch: Palestine and the Middle East 'peace process'★

International Socialism 2:71 Summer 1996
Chris Harman: The crisis of bourgeois economics ★ Hassan Mahamdallie: William Morris and revolutionary Marxism ★ Alex Callinicos: Darwin, materialism and revolution ★ Chris Nineham: Raymond Williams: revitalising the left? ★ Paul Foot: A passionate prophet of liberation ★ Gill Hubbard: Why has feminism failed women? ★ Lee Sustar: Bookwatch: fighting to unite black and white★

International Socialism 2:70 Spring 1996
Alex Callinicos: South Africa after apartheid ★ Chris Harman: France's hot December ★ Brian Richardson: The making of a revolutionary ★ Gareth Jenkins: Why Lucky Jim turned right—an obituary of Kingsley Amis ★ Mark O'Brien: The bloody birth of capitalism ★ Lee Humber: Studies in revolution ★ Adrian Budd: A new life for Lenin ★ Martin Smith: Bookwatch: the General Strike★

International Socialism 2:69 Winter 1995
Lindsey German: The Balkan war: can there be peace? ★ Duncan Blackie: The left and the Balkan war ★ Nicolai Gentchev: The myth of welfare dependency ★ Judy Cox: Wealth, poverty and class in Britain today ★ Peter Morgan: Trade unions and strikes ★ Julie Waterson: The party at its peak ★ Megan Trudell: Living to some purpose ★ Nick Howard: The rise and fall of socialism in one city ★ Andy Durgan: Bookwatch: Civil war and revolution in Spain ★

International Socialism 2:68 Autumn 1995
Ruth Brown: Racism and immigration in Britain ★ John Molyneux: Is Marxism deterministic? ★ Stuart Hood: News from nowhere? ★ Lee Sustar: Communism in the heart of the beast ★ Peter Linebaugh: To the teeth and forehead of our faults ★ George Paizis: Back to the future ★ Phil Marshall: The children of stalinism ★ Paul D'Amato: Bookwatch: 100 years of cinema ★

International Socialism 2:67 Summer 1995
Paul Foot: When will the Blair bubble burst? ★ Chris Harman: From Bernstein to Blair—100 years of revisionism ★ Chris Bambery: Was the Second World War a war for democracy? ★ Alex Callinicos: Hope against the Holocaust ★Chris Nineham: Is the media all powerful? ★ Peter Morgan: How the West was won ★ Charlie Hore: Bookwatch: China since Mao ★

International Socialism 2:66 Spring 1995
Dave Crouch: The crisis in Russia and the rise of the right ★ Phil Gasper: Cruel and unusual punishment: the politics of crime in the United States ★ Alex Callinicos: Backwards to liberalism ★ John Newsinger: Matewan: film and working class struggle ★ John Rees: The light and the dark ★ Judy Cox: How to make the Tories disappear ★ Charlie Hore: Jazz: a reply to the critics ★ Pat Riordan: Bookwatch: Ireland ★

International Socialism 2:65 Special issue
Lindsey German: Frederick Engels: life of a revolutionary ★ John Rees: Engels' Marxism ★ Chris Harman: Engels and the origins of human society ★ Paul McGarr: Engels and natural science ★

International Socialism 2:63 Summer 1994
Alex Callinicos: Crisis and class struggle in Europe today ★ Duncan Blackie: The United Nations and the politics of imperialism ★ Brian Manning: The English Revolution and the transition from

feudalism to capitalism ★ Lee Sustar: The roots of multi-racial labour unity in the United States ★ Peter Linebaugh: Days of villainy: a reply to two critics ★ Dave Sherry: Trotsky's last, greatest struggle ★ Peter Morgan: Geronimo and the end of the Indian wars ★ Dave Beecham: Ignazio Silone and *Fontamara* ★ Chris Bambery: Bookwatch: understanding fascism ★

International Socialism 2:62 Spring 1994
Sharon Smith: Mistaken identity—or can identity politics liberate the oppressed? ★ Iain Ferguson: Containing the crisis—crime and the Tories ★ John Newsinger: Orwell and the Spanish Revolution ★ Chris Harman: Change at the first millenium ★ Adrian Budd: Nation and empire—Labour's foreign policy 1945-51 ★ Gareth Jenkins: Novel questions ★ Judy Cox: Blake's revolution ★ Derek Howl: Bookwatch: the Russian Revolution ★

International Socialism 2:61 Winter 1994
Lindsey German: Before the flood? ★ John Molyneux: The 'politically correct' controversy ★ David McNally: E P Thompson—class struggle and historical materialism ★ Charlie Hore: Jazz—a people's music ★ Donny Gluckstein: Revolution and the challenge of labour ★ Charlie Kimber: Bookwatch: the Labour Party in decline ★

International Socialism 2:59 Summer 1993
Ann Rogers: Back to the workhouse ★ Kevin Corr and Andy Brown: The labour aristocracy and the roots of reformism ★ Brian Manning: God, Hill and Marx ★ Henry Maitles: Cutting the wire: a criticial appraisal of Primo Levi ★ Hazel Croft: Bookwatch: women and work ★

International Socialism 2:58 Spring 1993
Chris Harman: Where is capitalism going? (part one) ★ Ruth Brown and Peter Morgan: Politics and the class struggle today: a roundtable discussion ★ Richard Greeman: The return of Comrade Tulayev: Victor Serge and the tragic vision of Stalinism ★ Norah Carlin: A new English revolution ★ John Charlton: Building a new world ★ Colin Barker: A reply to Dave McNally ★

International Socialism 2:56 Autumn 1992
Chris Harman: The Return of the National Question ★ Dave Treece: Why the Earth Summit failed ★ Mike Gonzalez: Can Castro survive? ★ Lee Humber and John Rees: The good old cause—an interview with Christopher Hill ★ Ernest Mandel: The Impasse of Schematic Dogmatism ★

International Socialism 2:55 Summer 1992
Alex Callinicos: Race and class ★ Lee Sustar: Racism and class struggle in the American Civil War era ★ Lindsey German and Peter Morgan: Prospects for socialists—an interview with Tony Cliff ★ Robert Service: Did Lenin lead to Stalin? ★ Samuel Farber: In defence of democratic revolutionary socialism ★ David Finkel: Defending 'October' or sectarian dogmatism? ★ Robin Blackburn: Reply to John Rees ★ John Rees: Dedicated followers of fashion ★ Colin Barker: In praise of custom ★ Sheila McGregor: Revolutionary witness ★

International Socialism 2:54 Spring 1992
Sharon Smith: Twilight of the American dream ★ Mike Haynes: Class and crisis—the transition in eastern Europe ★ Costas Kossis: A miracle without end? Japanese capitalism and the world economy ★ Alex Callinicos: Capitalism and the state system: A reply to Nigel Harris ★ Steven Rose: Do animals have rights? ★ John Charlton: Crime and class in the 18th century ★ John Rees: Revolution, reform and working class culture ★ Chris Harman: Blood simple ★

International Socialism 2:51 Summer 1991
Chris Harman: The state and capitalism today ★ Alex Callinicos: The end of nationalism? ★ Sharon Smith: Feminists for a strong state? ★ Colin Sparks and Sue Cockerill: Goodbye to the Swedish miracle ★ Simon Phillips: The South African Communist Party and the South African working class ★ John Brown: Class conflict and the crisis of feudalism ★

International Socialism 2:49 Winter 1990
Chris Bambery: The decline of the Western Communist Parties ★ Ernest Mandel: A theory which has not withstood the test of time ★ Chris Harman: Criticism which does not withstand the test of logic ★ Derek Howl: The law of value In the USSR ★ Terry Eagleton: Shakespeare and the class struggle ★ Lionel Sims: Rape and pre-state societies ★ Sheila McGregor: A reply to Lionel Sims ★

International Socialism 2:48 Autumn 1990
Lindsey German: The last days of Thatcher ★ John Rees: The new imperialism ★ Neil Davidson and Donny Gluckstein: Nationalism and the class struggle in Scotland ★ Paul McGarr: Order out of chaos ★

International Socialism 2:46 Winter 1989
Chris Harman: The storm breaks ★ Alex Callinicos: Can South Africa be reformed? ★ John Saville: Britain, the Marshall Plan and the Cold War ★ Sue Clegg: Against the stream ★ John Rees: The rising bourgeoisie ★

International Socialism 2:44 Autumn 1989
Charlie Hore: China: Tiananmen Square and after ★ Sue Clegg: Thatcher and the welfare state ★ John Molyneux: *Animal Farm* revisited ★ David Finkel: After Arias, is the revolution over? ★ John Rose: Jews in Poland ★

International Socialism 2:41 Winter 1988
Polish socialists speak out: Solidarity at the Crossroads ★ Mike Haynes: Nightmares of the market ★ Jack Robertson: Socialists and the unions ★ Andy Strouthous: Are the unions in decline? ★ Richard Bradbury: What is Post-Structuralism? ★ Colin Sparks: George Bernard Shaw ★

International Socialism 2:39 Summer 1988
Chris Harman and Andy Zebrowski: Glasnost, before the storm ★ Chanie Rosenberg: Labour and the fight against fascism ★ Mike Gonzalez: Central America after the Peace Plan ★ Ian Birchall: Raymond Williams ★ Alex Callinicos: Reply to John Rees ★

International Socialism 2:35 Summer 1987
Pete Green: Capitalism and the Thatcher years ★ Alex Callinicos: Imperialism, capitalism and the state today ★ Ian Birchall: Five years of *New Socialist* ★ Callinicos and Wood debate 'Looking for alternatives to reformism' ★ David Widgery replies on 'Beating Time' ★

International Socialism 2:30 Autumn 1985
Gareth Jenkins: Where is the Labour Party heading? ★ David McNally: Debt, inflation and the rate of profit ★ Ian Birchall: The terminal crisis in the British Communist Party ★ replies on Women's oppression and *Marxism Today* ★

International Socialism 2:26 Spring 1985
Pete Green: Contradictions of the American boom ★ Colin Sparks: Labour and imperialism ★ Chris Bambery: Marx and Engels and the unions ★ Sue Cockerill: The municipal road to socialism ★ Norah Carlin: Is the family part of the superstructure? ★ Kieran Allen: James Connolly and the 1916 rebellion ★

International Socialism 2:18 Winter 1983
Donny Gluckstein: Workers' councils in Western Europe ★ Jane Ure Smith: The early Communist press in Britain ★ John Newsinger: The Bolivian Revolution ★ Andy Durgan: Largo Caballero and Spanish socialism ★ M Barker and A Beezer: Scarman and the language of racism ★

International Socialism 2:14 Winter 1981
Chris Harman: The riots of 1981 ★ Dave Beecham: Class struggle under the Tories ★ Tony Cliff: Alexandra Kollontai ★ L James and A Paczuska: Socialism needs feminism ★ reply to Cliff on Zetkin ★ Feminists In the labour movement ★